a prescription for a healthier, happier *life*

MATTHEW SLEETH, MD

TYNDALE
MOMENTUM™

The nonfiction imprint of
Tyndale House Publishers, Inc.

Visit Tyndale online at www.tyndale.com.

Visit Tyndale Momentum online at www.tyndalemomentum.com.

TYNDALE, *Tyndale Momentum*, and Tyndale's quill logo are registered trademarks of Tyndale House Publishers, Inc. The Tyndale Momentum logo is a trademark of Tyndale House Publishers, Inc. Tyndale Momentum is the nonfiction imprint of Tyndale House Publishers, Inc., Carol Stream, Illinois.

24/6: A Prescription for a Healthier, Happier Life

Designed by Daniel Farrell

Edited by Jonathan Schindler

Published in association with the literary agency of Daniel Literary Group, Nashville, TN.

For information about special discounts for bulk purchases, please contact Tyndale House Publishers at csresponse@tyndale.com, or call 1-800-323-9400.

Library of Congress Cataloging-in-Publication Data

Sleeth, Matthew, date.
  24/6 : a prescription for a healthier, happier life / Matthew Sleeth.
    p. cm.
  ISBN 978-1-4143-7228-0 (sc)
1. Sunday. 2. Sabbath. 3. Rest—Religious aspects—Christianity. 4. Time management—Religious aspects—Christianity. I. Title.
  BV111.3.S54 2012
  263′.3—dc23   2012025053

Printed in the United States of America

23   22   21   20   19   18   17
14   13   12   11   10   9   8

A Sabbath Poem

Breathe

rest in Rest,
holy Leisure—
airtight Time:

Sabbath.

hearing Ears,
Creation slowing—
open Eyes:

Sabbath.

guiltless Feasting,
sacred Rhythms—
Heaven Hugging:

Sabbath.

Nothing-doing
Nowhere-going—
Work unknowing:

Sabbath.

John David Walt,
ASBURY THEOLOGICAL SEMINARY

Contents

Foreword

THE SUBJECT OF Sabbath keeping is in the air these days. I think I have read with admiration and appreciation most of the books and articles written on this subject in the last fifty years. Maybe you have too. No matter—you must read this latest entry in the genre. Matthew Sleeth has crafted a compelling invitation to consider and participate in Sabbath keeping, an invitation that is, in my experience, without peer.

His credentials are impressive. His years of experience as an ER physician in hospitals qualifies him as a veteran in a culture of demanding overwork. His entry into the Christian faith ten years ago provides a total reorientation of his imagination in the Hebrew/Christian culture of Sabbath keeping. And most impressive of all, he explores the many details of what is involved in practicing Sabbath in a world that is unrelenting in its distractions and pressures to work longer and harder. He does it not as an impersonal "expert" but firmly in the context of marriage and family, with all the domestic and relational details involved in doing nothing where doing nothing always requires constant coordination and relationship.

Under Dr. Sleeth's pen, *Sabbath*, a dead word for so many, undergoes a resurrection, comes alive—not as a bare commandment, the fourth in the sequence of ten, but as a vigorous way to live in the present. This takes place in a freshly imagined (but not fanciful) recovery of the salvation and Jesus-context of the Scriptures. The writer's mastery of the entire biblical revelation raises Sabbath keeping far above an unadorned rule to be kept. In detail after detail it comes to be seen as a cornerstone for comprehending a world defined in all its daily living by God's rest, God's not-doing. He showcases Jesus' recovery of Sabbath keeping unfettered by the legalistic restrictions that had taken all the creativity and joy out of Sabbath in the world in which Jesus grew up. Jesus is still the primary antidote to the cheerless rule keeping associated with Sabbath in our time.

Which is to say that this is a book that restores Sabbath to its extensive biblical narrative context. Jesus, not rules, sets the tone. This Sabbath keeping is conveyed in stories— doctor stories, stories of friends, stories of family, Jesus stories. The stories keep Sabbath "nested"—integral to the time and place in which relationships form and develop. Everything is written in ways that give men and women dignity and room, atmosphere and space to be themselves in a good creation. There is not a hint of judgmentalism against any who are either unaware of or hostile to this holy day.

Sabbath is simply presented not as a rule to be kept but as a freedom to enter into.

Not the least of the attractions of *24/6* is the style of the writing—with wit, sharply observed phrasings, new ways to express old truths. Dr. Sleeth renames Sabbath "Stop Day." And here are a few sentences that stopped me in my tracks:

If the Ten Commandments are written on apple pie and you get to choose which slice to have based upon size, choose the fourth. You will get more than a third of the pie put on your plate.

No one ever found the Lord on the day they won the lottery. Faith is more likely to blossom on the day we lose our job.

Stopping and resting are the working definitions of holy.

The seventh day is blessed as holy because the Lord stopped and rested.

And here is a meditative practice that I find attractive. Until now I'd never come across subtracting one word at a time from Psalm 46:10 to help me come to rest:

Be still and know that I am God.
Be still and know that I am.

Be still and know that I.
Be still and know that.
Be still and know.
Be still and.
Be still.
Be.

The cumulative effect on me of this extended, comprehensive, and lively writing on Sabbath practice is a sense of how natural and inevitable it seems: *Yes, of course,* this *is the way we have been created to live well.* There is nothing obtrusive here, nothing that feels like an invasion of our privacy or an infringement of our "pursuit of happiness." That is not to say that the difficulties we face in Sabbath practice in our culture are not formidable obstructions to how we embrace the practice. Edmund Burke is often quoted saying, "Beware the terrible simplifiers." There is none of that here. But neither are there any onerous "Sabbath burdens" placed on us. In Sabbath keeping we become more ourselves, not less. In Dr. Sleeth's pithy sentence, "Sabbath is a time to transition from human doings to human beings."

Eugene H. Peterson
PROFESSOR EMERITUS OF SPIRITUAL THEOLOGY
REGENT COLLEGE
VANCOUVER, BC

From the Author

WHEN DAVID GREEN built his first craft store in 1972, his initial plan was to close his stores on Sundays so that his employees and their families, as well as his customers, could take the day off. But he got scared. A competitor vowed to drive him out of business, and one of his tactics was to operate seven days a week. So David opened on Sundays to match the competition.

As the years went by, his business thrived and expanded. He gave money to charity and to the church, but his conscience bothered him. With one hand he was supporting the church, and with the other he was working against it—literally. For many of his employees, Sunday was the only time they could go to church or spend time with their children. We've all heard the saying, "The customer is always right." This seems like sound business advice, and everything about David's approach to retailing honored this axiom. But something else worked on his conscience. A voice said, "*I* come before your customers."

Two decades after he began his business, David looked at the numbers. Hour for hour, Sunday had become his most profitable day of the week. He was selling a hundred million dollars in merchandise per year just on Sundays.

David prayed, and then he took the plunge. He decided to permanently close his stores on Sundays. "And that's when our business really took off," he said of his Hobby Lobby chain.

David's story is dramatic because of the numbers. But it is no less dramatic to be a single parent without enough hours in the day, or a college student with a big exam on Monday, or a child facing a Little League playoff on Sunday—and decide to live 24/6. Honoring the Sabbath is not only an act of faith these days; it is an act of courage.

Genesis opens with the Lord speaking the universe into existence. After each day, the Lord said, "Good." When you and I were formed, the Lord said, "Very good." Yet when the Sabbath was created, the Lord whispered, "Holy."

We live in the most fast-paced period of history. People literally fly from one continent to another. We cure diseases that have plagued every generation before us. The phone in my pocket has a medical library, a camera, and a thousand songs on board. These are incredible times, and yet I would not be able to make sense of them without my weekly Sabbath.

In writing *24/6*, I have tried to be honest. I have drawn from the truth of the Bible and from the stories of thousands of patients I saw as a doctor. I have changed names, places, and times when needed to maintain my oath of confidentiality. But I have tried to tell the truth as I know it.

I am still learning what God meant when he said, "Remember the Sabbath day, to keep it holy" (Exodus 20:8, ESV). My prayer is that this book will serve as a road map to some of the most wonderful places I've ever traveled—one Sunday at a time.

PART 1

Our 24/7 World

Take Time to Be Holy

Take time to be holy, speak oft with thy Lord;
Abide in Him always, and feed on His Word.
Make friends of God's children; help those who are weak,
Forgetting in nothing His blessing to seek.

Take time to be holy, the world rushes on;
Spend much time in secret with Jesus alone.
By looking to Jesus, like Him thou shalt be;
Thy friends in thy conduct His likeness shall see.

Take time to be holy, let Him be thy guide;
And run not before Him whatever betide.
In joy or in sorrow still follow thy Lord,
And, looking to Jesus, still trust in His Word.

Take time to be holy, be calm in thy soul;
Each thought and each motive beneath His control.
Thus led by His Spirit to fountains of love,
Thou soon shalt be fitted for service above.

William D. Longstaff

CHAPTER 1

What Is Missing *Does* Matter

As we keep or break the Sabbath day, we nobly save or
meanly lose the last best hope by which man rises.

Abraham Lincoln

SIX OF US stood around a translucent, illuminated X-ray
view screen. We were third-year medical students, and our
overall knowledge of the basic sciences would never be
better. We had mastered anatomy, pathology, physiology,
and pharmacology. We knew everything about medicine—
in theory.

Now we were ready for our first lesson in radiology. So
we took a deep breath, squared our shoulders, and stared at
the front and side views of the chest X-rays on the screen.

"See anything amiss?" the radiologist asked.

Quiet.

"Well, if you don't see anything wrong, does anyone care to comment on what's right?"

Still more quiet.

"Okay, let's start with the basics. Who can tell me the sex of the patient?"

And so he began teaching us the fundamentals of reading an X-ray. *It* was a *she*, twenty to forty years of age. The diaphragm was normal, the heart was not enlarged. No infections could be seen in the lungs. We couldn't see any tumors. After half an hour of tutelage, we were really getting the hang of radiology.

Then our professor began with some less obvious questions.

"Has she ever had chest trauma?"

Vacant stares.

"Does she have a partially collapsed lung?"

Whoops, forgot to look for that.

Lynn, the smallest of us and the one with the most pluck, interrupted the silence with the next best thing to an intelligent answer: "What is the history?"

"Good question. Cough for a few days. No fever. No chills. No weight loss or gain. No night sweats."

Nothing in the patient's history suggested anything other than a garden-variety cold.

Then we were asked to consider more subtle matters.

"Is she right- or left-handed? What kind of work does she do?"

Maybe there was a reason this fellow chaired the

department. We asked one another questions and thought of every obscure disease we had studied. For fleeting moments, each of us even saw evidence of various maladies. Finally, the X-ray held no secrets.

"Is there anything else, or did we get it all?" the radiologist asked.

An hour's worth of looking had confirmed what our textbooks said was the hardest kind of X-ray to be certain of: a normal one. We'd gotten the point. A lesson had been learned. Our teacher moved to put the films away.

We looked at one another with newfound confidence. We'd gone from being mute to being able to describe subtleties. If we'd been better at eye–hand coordination and duller at memorizing, we might have given one another high fives.

As we turned toward lunch, our mentor spoke one last time. "This film was read by the doctor in charge of the emergency department last night—and the radiology resident on call last night and the one this morning—and they all agreed with you. But I called the patient to tell her I think she has cancer."

We forgot about lunch and turned back to the X-rays. Again we stared at the films, but we couldn't see any evidence of cancer, even as we tried to talk ourselves into it. We looked and looked, but to no avail.

"I'll give you a hint," he said. "It's not something there but something *missing* that bothers me."

Even with this clue, we came up blank. And we really

tried. We pointed to one thing after another, but each time the radiologist would shake his head no.

Someone's stomach rumbled. We were tired and hungry and ready to admit defeat. Our teacher mercifully gave away the answer in his final question: "Where is the left clavicle?"

Where was the left clavicle? It was missing. We hadn't seen it because it wasn't there. The patient's collarbone had been eaten away, almost certainly by cancer.

The take-home point? What's missing *does* matter.

Something Missing

As a medical student and resident, I routinely worked a ridiculous number of hours. But you don't have to go to medical school to feel like your life is out of control. Whether we are doctors, lawyers, or Indian chiefs, most of us today work too much. Schoolteachers can't leave any child behind, truckers have logbooks, and camp directors need advanced degrees to run a ropes challenge course. It seems as if everyone is working harder. Nobody has a three-martini lunch. There's no time left to sleep on the job. We are all too busy.

And we don't just work at one thing anymore. We drink coffee and drive cars. We drive cars and talk on the phone. We talk on the phone and shop in the cloud . . . and fix dinner . . . and watch the news.

In the last twenty years, work is up 15 percent and

leisure is down 30 percent, and things are only going to get worse. Yet statistics tell only part of the story. They don't account for multitasking, nor do they reflect leisure time per entire family unit. Mom works two jobs, and so do Dad and Sis. Junior is in kindergarten, and he no longer takes a nap after lunch or goes home in the afternoon, as I did. He is in school all day, and if the bureaucrats have their way, Junior and Sis will soon lose their summer vacation.

When I was growing up during the baby boom, everyone was fascinated by the future. Films, books, and cartoons were filled with optimistic predictions. The Jetsons' robot did the laundry and cooked meals as aerocars whizzed through clean, blue skies. While tourists ogled displays at the 1964 World's Fair, sociologists began to predict that too much spare time might become a problem. How would everyone cope with a three-day workweek and four months of vacation every year?

Half a century later, these are moot questions. Too much leisure time is far from the reality that most people experience today. As the announcer on the Epcot ride intones, "The future is now!" We have robots, computers, and time-saving gadgets galore, but the promise of too much time on our hands hasn't materialized. In fact, most of us seem busier than ever. "There aren't enough hours in the day" is a common complaint. If the past fifty years have a lesson to teach, it is this: one more piece of technology will bring neither more time nor more happiness. Despite a plethora of robotic vacuums, electric clothes dryers, and three-minute eggs cooked in thirty seconds, something seems to be missing.

The Misplaced Day

Remember what the radiologist taught? It is hard to see something that's not there. Something *is* missing from our lives—something that until now had been safely passed along, generation upon generation.

Just a short while ago, almost everything in society stopped one day a week. Gas stations, banks, and grocery stores locked their doors at night and on Sundays. No more. We are no longer a society that goes to sleep at night or conducts business six days a week. Now we go 24/7. And in the metamorphosis to a 24/7 world, something, like the clavicle in the X-ray, has gone missing.

What got taken away is rest. Sunday was the day when libraries and pharmacies barred the door and people got dressed up and drove to church. Those without particular religious convictions simply took the day off. Jews marked Saturday as their holy day and called it *Sabbath*. Seventh-day Adventists did likewise. Most Baptist, Methodist, and Presbyterian clergy relaxed on Mondays. Irrespective of faith, all members of society were given and even guaranteed a day each week when they could rest.

Subtracting a day of rest each week has had a profound effect on our lives. How could it not? One day a week adds up. Fifty-two days a year times an average life span is equal to more than eleven years. Take away eleven years of anything in a lifetime, and there will be a change. This is a law of the universe: for every action, there is an equal and opposite reaction. Subtract over a decade of sleep, work, or education, and the entire character of one's existence is altered. Multiply eleven years times a third of a billion Americans, and you are looking for a lost continent of time. Unfortunately, in our society, it's not Monday that got mislaid; it's our Sabbath, our day of rest. If there is to be any hope for recovering the Sabbath, we must first admit that something is missing. Despite reassurances of convenience, safety, and choice, America has been conned. My generation was raised with a day off each week. We witnessed the change to 24/7; we saw a cultural treasure stolen. Still, there was no outcry. It happened so quickly, and yet so gradually, that no one even protested. And now my children's generation does not have

Unfortunately, in our society, it's not Monday that got mislaid; it's our Sabbath, our day of rest.

a day of rest at all. The song lyric "you don't know what you've got till it's gone" is only partially true. If you've never seen something, how do you know it's missing?

A weekly day of rest is like Cherry Garcia ice cream and hugs: we can survive without them, but we can't really live. I once asked an auditorium full of grade-school children sitting on bleachers about a weekly day of rest. "What do you think about everyone stopping one day a week? No chores. No homework. No parents going off to work. No shopping. No errands. Does this sound like a good idea?" They stared, smiling at me like I was asking if it was okay to add another Christmas to the year, or if any of them would mind being able to fly.

Suppose that everyone got to take off one day a week. No one cheated. Six days a week is all any business could or would operate. If you're open for business on Sunday, you have to close one other day of the week. If you're closed on Saturdays, then you can operate Sundays. You get the idea. For the moment, put aside concerns about hospitals and emergencies and that sort of thing; we are simply considering what would be ideal. Everyone in the country works only six days a week. That's the rule.

In a highly unscientific survey I conduct by asking people (when I remember), 100 percent of the respondents I've asked so far are in favor of this plan. It is ironic that if polled, 100 percent of Americans would say they believe that no one should steal, lie, or cheat. Keep in mind that there are many things people will not agree upon. Country, rap, and classical music are examples: some people love them, some not so much. But when everyone agrees on something and yet that something does not exist, be assured that we are dealing with the most important issues in the solar system. We are dealing with the deepest business of humanity.

A day of rest is missing from our lives, and as in the case

of the X-ray, what is missing is hard to see. To the radiologist, the missing clavicle was a sign of illness. As a barefoot theologian, I regard the missing day of rest as a worrisome sign.

The practice of stopping one day a week—of only going 24/6—is not new for humanity. It started the day after human history began, and it made it through the decline and fall of the Roman Empire. It didn't perish when it was exported to the New World. It survived the American Civil War and was still going strong when women got the vote. It prospered in the Depression, and it blasted off at the dawn of the Space Age. Only in the last few minutes of time has it been misplaced.

But where did our day of rest go—and can we live without it?

CHAPTER 2

Remember the Sabbath

*Remember that you were once slaves in Egypt, but the
LORD your God brought you out with his strong hand
and powerful arm. That is why the LORD your God
has commanded you to rest on the Sabbath day.*

Deuteronomy 5:15

HUMAN MEMORY is complicated. I learned how tricky
it can be one January morning while on duty at a hospital in Maine. It was a few hours before the sun came up.
A patient arrived at the hospital by ambulance. The air
was dry and still. Stars burned in the sky overhead and
reflected off the snow-covered landscape. The ambulance
crew opened the one-and-a-half story automatic door of
the emergency room bay, triggering two long banks of pro-
pane heaters that blazed to life along the ceiling. The job of
the heaters was to bring the air up thirty degrees to at least
zero. Intense cold can slow down a diesel engine or stop an

old heart. The crew tracked snow and salt across the floor
with their L. L. Bean boots as they unwrapped Mrs. Bebe
from a cocoon of blankets and gently placed her in bed C,
which is where heart cases go.

Mrs. Bebe was an alert woman who thanked several of
the rescue squad members by name. She had a kind of glow
about her, as they say. She'd lived long enough to see the
collision of two epochs. The heroes of her day had thrown
themselves on land mines and foreign beaches. She'd
learned to read in a one-room school and worn a hand-
made dress. Decades of hardship had made her better, not
bitter.

One gets a clue of a patient's social landscape by observing who scrapes off the windshield and drives to the ER at
5:00 a.m. to see her. Mostly those hours are a lonely vigil
for the sick. Not so for this woman. Sons, daughters, and
grandchildren arrived in respectful quiet and sensible dress.
These visitors were not drawn to Mrs. Bebe because of her
money or position but because of that most subtle of forces
that binds hearts together.

I introduced myself to her and asked what had brought
her to the ER. "I woke up hurting right here," she said as
she clenched her fist and motioned in a circle over the area
where the heart inhabits the chest. I listened to the *lub-dub*
emanating from her heart and then to her breathing. After
examining her, I ordered a cardiogram, a chest X-ray, and
the usual battery of tests. The EKG was normal: no signs of
anything untoward. The portable chest X-ray was normal.

The first lab tests came back normal—actually, better than normal; I would have gladly traded cholesterol levels with her. "Hmmm," I said. (We doctors are prone to falling back on technical terms such as this when we are not quite sure what is going on.) With the lab results in hand, I went out to the waiting room and told the family that so far everything was looking good and that we would wait for the rest of the labs to come back before deciding on a course of action.

Her family was anxious to see for themselves that she was okay, so the nurse led them back a few at a time. The waiting room was looking more crowded and congenial. Some of the well-wishers made plans to get children off to school. Everyone volunteered in any way they could. "Take my blood . . . kidney . . . whatever you need; we're here to help" was their collective response.

I was sitting at the desk in my office when Mrs. Bebe's medical record arrived. It was thin for someone her age. As a rule, I am not quick at recognizing patterns in numbers, but this time I spotted one. She'd been to the hospital on few occasions, but when she did show up, it was always in the middle of the first month of the year. The diagnosis was listed various times as "atypical chest pain," "noncardiac chest pain," or "rule out MI." She'd been admitted on several occasions, and each examination had uncovered nothing serious. Mrs. Bebe didn't impress me as a complainer. Still, why the nonevents? She wasn't a smoker or drinker. She didn't have any allergies or even take any medicines on a regular basis. Under the social history, there was a note explaining that she lived alone with a close-knit social support network nearby. She'd been listed as widowed since the earliest part of the record.

I went back to talk with the patient. Her son and granddaughter stood by the bed. "I see in your patient record that you lost your husband. Do you mind me asking how he passed away?" There was a pause, and the question seemed to float in the air, taking on a life of its own. Somehow I'd stumbled into this family's elephant in the living room. The granddaughter looked like a graffiti artist caught in high beams.

There was more silence, and then Mrs. Bebe spoke. "It was after the war," she began. "It was on a night as cold as this. We were all asleep. My husband heard it first. The animals were bawling. He called to the children and then ran to the barn to get the cows out. The barn was on fire." One of the peculiarities of rural New England architecture is that many barns and houses are joined together by a low structure called an *ell*. This configuration allows for the multiple daily trips from kitchen to milking stanchions during seasons when twelve-foot drifts of snow cover the ground. The downside is that as goes the barn, so goes the house.

The son filled in where his mother had left off. In broad strokes, he painted the picture of a woman standing in the snow, huddled with five children, praying for a husband who never returned. The house, the way of life, the wedding dress, the family Bible with its record of hatched, matched, and dispatched—everything was lost.

Mrs. Bebe had lost her husband in the middle of January. Now, more than half a century later, she had woken out of sleep with a pain in her chest. Neither the patient nor her family had ever connected the dots. We doctors had ordered tests and ruled out heart attacks, but we'd also managed to miss the point. A simple connection had been overlooked. Mrs. Bebe's heart wasn't diseased; it was broken.

The link between Mrs. Bebe's tragic anniversary, her broken heart, and her aching chest came together by luck one night, but how many similar connections escape us every day? Such patterns often go unnoticed—in medicine, in families, and in life. That is the way of humankind. We are clever, but we forget.

Our memory and our vision are often least reliable when it comes to the things we are closest to and care about the most. We are often the last ones to see what is obvious to an outsider. Haven't we all known a child who everyone can clearly see is spoiled—except the child's parents? If saintly Mrs. Bebe and her family had forgotten the tragedy that defined them, how is society to keep track of all seven days in a week? Maybe it isn't so much dark intentions that resulted in the loss of Sabbath as it is a kind of society-wide absentmindedness. Maybe that is why the commandment about the Sabbath is the only one of the Ten Commandments that begins with the word *remember*.

Marking Time

God whispered, "Begin, sweet world," and time began. Adam and Eve walked in the Garden. They had no wristwatches. They had no calendar. There was evening, night, and then another day, and then another and another. The Bible preserves the mysteries of the couple's marriage. One might mistakenly assume that their honeymoon only lasted a short while, but it wouldn't have been paradise if that were the case. Imagine: no death, no taxes; nothing but years and years of, well, paradise stretching out in front of you.

Then the market crashed. Sin came into the world. The honeymooners had to deal with traffic, airport security lines, you name it. It wasn't hell, but it wasn't paradise, either. The animals were fair game. Adam got a day job. At night he surfed channels and sipped scotch. Eve went to bed in a flannel nightgown.

Some dismiss Genesis, but it rings true. We feel the gist of it in our bones: Something went terribly wrong. Something is missing.

Some dismiss Genesis, but it rings true. We feel the gist of it in our bones: Something went terribly wrong. Something is missing.

This void persists even in the best of lives. It is why politicians hide mistresses and billionaires risk it all to get that second billion. This is the story of humanity. We find the perfect job and it goes away. We fall in love, and our hearts are broken.

After the crash, time no longer worked in humanity's favor. One morning, Adam woke, peered in the mirror, and realized his comb-over wasn't fooling anybody. The mainspring on Eve's bioclock unwound. They ached for the old days and avoided the subject of Abel. Life was brutish and short . . . and then death arrived. One day faded into another. What did time mean when one in seven moms died in childbirth and half the preschool class died before kindergarten? How did people keep track of time when they had so little of it? What is the right amount of time to have?

With the advent of electricity, time has new meaning. We are the first 24/7 society. We complain of too little time, yet our days are so full that many of us run out of memory before we reach the end of them.

I got a call yesterday. "Good news!" I was told. "You've been selected to receive a new home alarm system."

"Where are you calling from?" I asked the bearer of my windfall. He was in Mumbai. I thanked him but declined his generous offer. A phone solicitation to Kentucky at 5:00 p.m. means that someone is up at 3:30 a.m. in Mumbai. (That's right: many cities around the world are in half-hour time zones.) Is that before or after today?

The way we measure time is in many ways artificial and subjective. A calendar from the dentist in Afghanistan begins in March, not January. Two hundred years ago, every city established its own time by measuring the height of the sun at noon. Then, in the 1880s, trains forced vast regions of the United States into single time zones.

We take our seven-day week for granted, but the seven-day week is neither universal nor astronomical. Like time zones, it is arbitrary. The time it takes the Earth to make one complete trip around the sun is not an even number of days. Early societies were faced with a problem keeping track of the days. The sun rises and sets at different times depending on the season. The night sky reveals a moon's phases, but lunar cycles bear no relationship to the seasons, and forecasting the onset of spring and fall was of vital importance. It was crucial to be able to predict planting and harvest times.

If the average person awoke on a deserted island and had to start from scratch, he or she would be hard pressed to come up with the Pope Gregory version of the calendar hanging on your wall. Gregory's system replaced Julius Caesar's calendar, which had gone out of whack by ten days over 1,500 short years. Gregory's calendar is good, but it's not perfect. The days in the month are spread unevenly. One month could have gotten all the extra days, but instead we have, "Thirty days have September, April, June, and November . . ." Will Christmas fall on Monday or Tuesday this year? Can a person born on February 29 live four times longer?

Historians have struggled to reconcile one ancient calendar with another. At times, an astronomical event such as an eclipse or a geophysical event such as the eruption of a volcano will allow the syncing of various calendars. But the task is not easy. How does the first year of the Emperor

Galba sync up with the fourth year of King Artabunus's rule in a world that simultaneously kept five-, seven-, eight-, ten-, and twelve-day weeks? January 1 became New Year's Day one hundred and fifty years before the birth of Christ—and it has nothing to do with any astronomical event.

The Roman calendar of the year 46 BC contained 445 days. Our current year has 365.25 days. The Jewish year, because it follows lunar cycles, contains around 360 days. This necessitated adding four to six days from time to time. The good news is that the days the rabbis added weren't Mondays, but Sabbaths. To the Jews, the key principle at work is not a Sabbath day marching back in time till Creation, but having no more than six days of work in a row. Misplacing a few days just happens over the course of thousands of years. Who knows how many days are missing? And the current Jewish calendar, invented in the fourth century, is not the one Jesus used.

When Is the Sabbath?

All this raises a question: is the Sabbath day of this week the same as the one Moses observed long ago? The answer: there's at least a one-in-seven chance.

For those who hold that the Sabbath occurs on Saturday and that Saturday Sabbaths march back in seven-day increments to the beginning of time—I do not wish to dissuade you in any way. Celebrate the day you believe is ordained.

At some point in the early history of the church, Christians who simultaneously kept a Roman calendar *and* a Jewish one moved the weekly celebration of the Lord from the last day of the week to the first day of the week in relationship to the Hebrew calendar as it existed at that time. Instead of focusing exclusively on rest, the new Christians turned their attention to sharing a meal, the Lord's Supper. The day became known as the Lord's Day.

In observing a Sabbath and/or the Lord's Day, there has been much controversy. Churches have split, and people have literally been killed. This book cannot resolve the question of when to begin and end a Sabbath day. Even if the Earth went around the sun in even increments, and even if there were a perfect record of time since God started everything, and even if we knew the exact date that God spoke the universe into existence, we still wouldn't know where God was when he sat down for the first Sabbath. Was he in Mumbai or in Kentucky? Did the first Sabbath begin in one of Africa's five time zones, or maybe to the west in Manhattan? Was God on Saturn, the jewel of the solar system, when he put his feet up on the Earth? Even if we could answer these questions and resolve all the days added by rabbis, would we know when an astronaut in the International Space Station should begin the Sabbath?

The controversies dealing with when to observe the Sabbath point to the most important question: are we supposed to stop one out of every seven days and mark it as a holy day? The answer to *this* question is the one *24/6* is after.

Thus, for the purposes of this book, it doesn't matter what you call the Sabbath—Shabbat, Shabbos, Saturday, Sunday, 24/6, a day of rest, ceasing day, or Stop Day. What's important is the stopping.

What God Created on the Seventh Day

In Genesis, we find a seven-day week. On Monday, God cooks up a universe with a few simple ingredients. He mixes nuclear weak and strong forces with a dash of gravity and a pinch of electromagnetism. He seasons the mix with covalent and ionic bonds. By midweek, he forms the dry land and the seas and says, "Good." On Friday after coffee, he stocks the lakes and fills the sky with birds. By the day's end, he sits on the tailgate admiring a flock of starlings bursting in one direction like a cumulus cloud. Each day, the universe becomes more multifaceted and interdependent. Each day things get more complicated. On day six, God forms Adam, and then—because she is even more complicated—God makes Eve. "Yes! Excellent! Very good! *Tov m'od*!"

How can God top creating a universe and my wife and daughter?

The *pièce de résistance* comes out of left field. Up to this point, everything has been created out of nothing, but on the morning of the seventh day, God makes nothing out of something. Rest is brought into being.

To argue about the name of the day or the time of its

beginning or when it ends is to miss the point. The word *Sabbath* means "cease from working." The concept is holy. The ancient Hebrews did not have names for the days of the week; they had numbers: one day, two day, three day, four day, five day, six day, and stop day. But the name is not important; it's what happens on that day that matters. Resting one day a week by any name is holy—the point is to stop on that day and look for God.

Up to this point, everything has been created out of nothing, but on the morning of the seventh day, God makes nothing out of something. Rest is brought into being.

Did Adam and Eve take off on the Sabbath? Oddly, or perhaps very tellingly, the Bible doesn't say. Did they know they were working before the Fall? Whatever they once had is forever lost. The road to Eden is guarded by an impenetrable firewall. Still, many have sought to go back. People have tried drugs, drink, and romance. Others have tried power, politics, and luxury. We've attempted to blast through the gates with science, city planning, and rational thought. But in the end, we are left out on the stoop, ringing the bell of a door that does not open. Some conclude by this that God never existed in the first place, but for me the Sabbath is irrefutable proof that God is real. It is so sublime that no person—much less a committee—could have invented it.

In C. S. Lewis's last book of the Narnia series, a group of dwarfs sits on the ground, obstinately shouting, "The

Dwarfs are for the Dwarfs!" All the while they fail to notice that they are sitting before the open gates of heaven. Could it be that in our grief we are like Lewis's dwarfs, overlooking the greatest prize in the galaxy? Do we also fail to notice the Sabbath beckoning us onward and upward? If Moses and a wayward bunch of stiff-necks without Internet access could count on rest once a week but we can't, how smart does that make us?

We cannot turn back the hands of time. Our 24/7 world is not going to change. Life will only get more intense. New communication tools, nanotechnology, and human engineering will increase the number of tasks an individual can do simultaneously. We will look back with nostalgia at the 24/7 world once these "advances" make 48/7 a reality. If we wish to have a weekly day of rest, it will no longer happen as a societal default. It will happen only as a result of a conscious choice. All that we need to begin is to "remember," as the Fourth Commandment tells us. We must remember the why and how of a day of rest.

But memory is a funny thing. Much of human history has been about the struggle for memory. From the paintings on the cave walls in Chauvet, to the Rosetta Stone, to fountain pens, to computers and Wikipedia, we want to remember. "Remember the Sabbath" is how the longest of the Ten Commandments begins.

The Hebrews believed that if everyone kept the Sabbath for just one day, all would be set right in the universe. The gates to Eden would fall open, pollution wouldn't exist, sunspots and dandruff would disappear, and teens would insist on cleaning up after a meal. But consider the Sabbath a little closer to home: What would it look like if just you and your family *remembered*?

What would happen if the Lord whispered, "Begin, sweet Sabbath"—and you listened?

CHAPTER 3

How the Fourth Commandment Got Added, Multiplied, and Subtracted

What sorrow also awaits you experts in religious law! For you crush people with unbearable religious demands, and you never lift a finger to ease the burden.

Luke 11:46

BILL WATSON FLEW into town to interview for a management position at the manufacturing headquarters near the hospital where I was moonlighting. He went out to dinner with six others from the senior staff and enjoyed both the people and the conversation.

When his hosts dropped him off at his hotel around 9:30, he called his wife to tell her how well the process was going. He got ready for bed, brushed his teeth, and then hit a snag: he couldn't empty his bladder. After dinner, two glasses of wine, two glasses of water, and a cup of coffee, his bladder was full. The problem was his prostate.

The prostate is a gland that lives under a man's bladder.

There it bides its time, quietly going about its business for decades, all the while growing like the national debt. The 50-50 rule applies to this gland: by the time men reach their fifties, half will have an enlarged prostate—a condition known as benign prostatic hypertrophy, or BPH.

Certain substances make the prostate swell acutely. The alcohol Bill had with dinner caused his prostate to go into overdrive and contract around the tube that drains the bladder. This wasn't the first time something like this had happened. On two occasions before, he'd experienced a similar although much less dramatic effect after a glass of wine. In those instances, it had caused a traffic jam, not a complete gridlock. Once the alcohol wore off, he had been able to empty his bladder without any further problems.

Bill said he'd hesitated to have a drink, but he didn't want to seem prudish when his hosts were obviously enjoying themselves. What he had not figured into the equation was the cold medicine he'd taken before his flight. Together, they had brought his bladder's drainage system to a complete standstill.

Bill ignored his expanding bladder in hopes that it would soon right itself. He turned on the television. One show finished, and another went by. As the late news ended and *The Tonight Show* began, Bill once again tested the plumbing to see if it was working—but to no avail. He was getting really uncomfortable.

Bill checked the system during every commercial break throughout the *Late Late Show*. When the infomercials began, Bill knew he was in big trouble, but he was in too much agony to drive to the hospital and too embarrassed to call 911. What would he say when they asked about the nature of his problem? That he was about to explode?

Fortunately, Bill had an old friend at his prospective employer. He called and explained the situation. It took another half hour for the friend to arrive at the hotel. After the drive to the hospital, Bill could hardly stand, and he definitely could not sit.

I didn't know Bill Watson existed until the night-shift nurse rang the phone in the call room. The clock numbers glowed 3:47.

"This is Lois," announced the nurse in the ER. "I've got a fifty-seven-year-old man here who just needs his bladder cathed *and* I've got two BP cuffs that aren't working. I won't be able do the chart until I go out on the floor and get another blood pressure machine. I'll call you when I'm finished." Lois was a new nurse to me, but she seemed to be on top of things.

In the old days, the night nurse would have just cathed a patient like this and wouldn't have even bothered calling the doctor unless the patient needed to be admitted. Now, it was all about the paperwork. I'd need to chat with the patient and make sure he had follow-up care and then sign his chart, but really it was the nurse who was the hero in these cases.

I got out of the narrow bed, went to the bathroom, washed up, and headed to the ER. I detoured by the cafeteria to get a soda and poured it into a large coffee cup. (Hint to new doctors: nobody is reassured by a doctor sipping from a soda can, but drinking what appears to be black coffee is perfectly legit.)

When I sauntered into the deserted ER, Lois and the patient were nowhere to be found. *They must be up front in the procedure room.* I took a gulp of my soda, walked to the procedure room, knocked, and opened the door.

Bill Watson was a tough man, yet when I opened the door and saw him rocking and shifting back and forth by the exam table with tears rolling silently down his face, I saw a man ready to give up.

Two blood pressure machines were parked in disarray beside the patient bed. The chart was on the end of the bed, waiting to be filled out. My eyes must have gone wide when I realized that Lois had left this suffering man without putting a catheter in him so she could wander around looking for a machine to record his blood pressure.

Get a catheter in a man like Bill, drain his bladder, and you've got a friend for life. I like having friends. So that is exactly what I did.

The bladder wants to empty once it is filled with twelve ounces of fluid or less—about one soda can's worth. I drained eight soda cans' worth of fluid from Bill's bladder and was well on the way to a twelve pack when Lois finally walked back into the room triumphantly pushing a blood pressure machine. "Can you believe there weren't any working machines in the department? It was like pulling teeth to get the floor to give me one!" she crowed.

Looking for a portable blood pressure machine when what Bill needed was a catheter? Talk about not seeing the forest for the trees! Later, when Lois explained her thinking, she said she was taught not to initiate treatment without getting vital signs first. That makes sense, but the purpose of vital signs is to know what to treat, which in this case was excruciatingly obvious.

"If you didn't want to cath him without the vitals, why didn't you just call me to do it?" I asked.

"Because I knew you would want the vital signs." She was just doing her job—even if it killed Bill.

Lois's logic is an example of concrete thinking. The reasoning of a concrete thinker is locked in, rigid, and inflexible. We have all known people who seem to have a knack for not getting the point. They take the letter of the law and lose sight of the intent behind it. The Bible is replete with stories that illustrate this all-too-human propensity.

In *24/6*, we are looking for the intent behind the law. What is the objective of the Fourth Commandment? And can we learn something by reading about its origin?

We don't need to go far into the Bible to discover the origin of the Sabbath: it's right there on the first page.

How the Fourth Commandment Got Added

"Thus the heavens and the earth were finished, and all the host of them. And on the seventh day God finished his work that he had done, and he rested on the seventh day from all his work that he had done. So God blessed the seventh day and made it holy, because on it God rested from all his work that he had done in creation" (Genesis 2:1-3, ESV).

In the beginning of the greatest story ever told, we find the inventor of everything taking a rest and enjoying his creation. And like most of the first few chapters of Genesis, this isn't so much an explanation of *how*, but of *who*. The *who*, of course, is God.

Who spoke the light into shining and the earth into spinning and the creeping, crawling things into crawling? God! How? That's not the point. Imagine an infinite God creating for six infinitely glorious days, and then on the seventh day he rests. We don't know the details. Trying to puzzle them out might be a little like Lois wanting Bill's vital signs while Bill's bladder is about to go supernova.

God doesn't need to rest after creating the universe because he's tired. He rests because he is holy, and everything that God does is holy.

The point is that something very important about the character of God is revealed on the seventh day: God stops.

Stopping is a problem for humans. We get a comfortable house, and then we want a bigger one. We get enough to eat, and then we want more.

God doesn't need to rest after creating the universe because he's tired. He rests because he is holy, and everything that God does is holy. God rests. God is holy. Therefore, rest is holy. It's simple math.

Rest shows us *who* God is. He has restraint. Restraint is refraining from doing everything that one has the power to do. We must never mistake God's restraint for weakness. The opposite is true. God shows restraint; therefore, restraint is holy.

After its introduction at the start of Genesis, Sabbath doesn't show up in the Bible again until Exodus 16. Not one word about it through all the generations of begetting that started with Eve. No mention of it when the Flood comes, when God scatters the people of Babel, or when Abraham and Isaac make the most awkward ride home in history. Not so much as a "Shabbat shalom" when Joseph goes from riches to rags to riches. Four hundred years pass between the close of Genesis and the start of Exodus with nary a peep about anything—including the Sabbath.

When Exodus opens, four centuries have passed without a sign from God. The Hebrew people have gone from honored visitors in Egypt to slaves building warehouses for Pharaoh. When they complain, their work gets harder. The meaning of their lives is bricks, bricks, bricks—ten days a week. (The ancient Egyptian year was divided into three seasons with a three-week month and a ten-day week.) Then a hero comes on the scene: Moses is born.

God hears the cries of his people, and the battle for the Hebrews is on. Guess who wins? This is one of the pivotal moments in all of history, when God brings his people out of Egypt.

Now, when my children were growing up and I wanted

to talk to them about something important, I would either take them out to eat or else go for a drive. If the subject warranted, sometimes we did both. It's an eight-hour drive from Cairo to Jerusalem. It takes a week by donkey, and you can walk it in less than a month. But on the occasion of emancipating his people, God made a slight detour. He took them for a 14,600-day ride in the country.

Nothing improves the taste of dinner as much as missing lunch. Laying your head on the pillow is never more delightful than after completing a hard day's work. What better time to educate the human race about rest than after twenty generations of slavery?

What better way to teach dependence than to go to a place with no food or water?

What better time to learn monotheism than after living in a culture where you can have as many gods as you want—just cast them in a kiln?

What better way to demonstrate the illusion of Pharaoh's immortality than to make his body disappear in the sea?

For forty years, God feeds the people every meal, shades them during the day, and guides them like a GPS. A few months into the trip, the tribes of Israel pull up to the base of Mount Sinai, and Moses climbs up to have a few words with the Maker of the universe. During their epic journey, God gives the Hebrews a total of 613 laws. But here at Mount Sinai, God personally pens the Top Ten.

If the Ten Commandments are written on apple pie

and you get to choose which slice to have based upon size, choose the fourth. You will get more than a third of the pie put on your plate:

And God spoke all these words, saying,

[1] "I am the LORD your God, who brought you out of the land of Egypt, out of the house of slavery. You shall have no other gods before me.

[2] "You shall not make for yourself a carved image, or any likeness of anything that is in heaven above, or that is in the earth beneath, or that is in the water under the earth. You shall not bow down to them or serve them, for I the LORD your God am a jealous God, visiting the iniquity of the fathers on the children to the third and the fourth generation of those who hate me, but showing steadfast love to thousands of those who love me and keep my commandments.

[3] "You shall not take the name of the LORD your God in vain, for the LORD will not hold him guiltless who takes his name in vain.

[4] "Remember the Sabbath day, to keep it holy. Six days you shall labor, and do all your work, but the seventh day is a Sabbath to the LORD your God. On it you shall not do any work, you, or your son, or your daughter, your male servant, or your female servant, or your livestock, or the sojourner who is within your gates. For in six days the LORD made

heaven and earth, the sea, and all that is in them, and rested on the seventh day. Therefore the LORD blessed the Sabbath day and made it holy.

[5] "Honor your father and your mother, that your days may be long in the land that the LORD your God is giving you.

[6] "You shall not murder.

[7] "You shall not commit adultery.

[8] "You shall not steal.

[9] "You shall not bear false witness against your neighbor.

[10] "You shall not covet your neighbor's house; you shall not covet your neighbor's wife, or his male servant, or his female servant, or his ox, or his donkey, or anything that is your neighbor's." (Exodus 20:1-17, ESV)

The first three commandments concern themselves with our relationship with God. The last six have to do with our dealings with each other. We cannot steal from, lie to, or kill God, but we can do these things to one another.

The Fourth Commandment is the longest and most inclusive of all ten. Its placement is not by accident. The first three commandments are about God; the last six are about humanity. The fourth acts as a fulcrum. It is a bridge between the two sections. The Sabbath commandment embraces the wealthy, the slave, and the illegal immigrant. It pertains to minimum-wage workers and to students. It covers animals. It includes children. The Fourth Commandment applies equally to men and women. It is made to protect those who believe and those who do not. It is to be followed by humanity, and it is observed by God himself.

Thousands of years ago, the trumpets sounded and the wind blew. God stood on a mountain and spoke to a band of frightened refugees. The people were rescued from centuries of slavery. An agreement was made between heaven and earth: "You must keep the Sabbath day, for it is a holy day for you. Anyone who desecrates it must be put to death; anyone who works on that day will be cut off from the community" (Exodus 31:14). The covenant was like a marriage agreement between God and his people. Breaking the Sabbath would be akin to a wife taking off her wedding band and throwing it in her husband's face on national television. How odd it must have been for those desert sojourners adjusting to life under the one true God. Before, they built statues of deities resembling birds, cattle, and reptiles. Now they followed the God with no earthly likeness, one who could not be cast in gold or carved in stone. They had labored for a pharaoh whose name they cursed, and now they ate from the hand of God, whose name was so sacred it must not be spoken.

The Fourth Commandment applies equally to men and women. It is made to protect those who believe and those who do not. It is to be followed by humanity, and it is observed by God himself.

The Hebrew people had worked 24/7 under task-masters, and now they put everything on hold once a week. They had borne discrimination, but now they were charged with protecting the interests of aliens, strangers, and orphans. They had come from a place that murdered infant boys, and now they were instructed to dedicate newborns to the Lord. Thou shalt not murder, commit adultery, steal, or lie—these they understood; most of the time Egyptians followed these rules too. But don't envy? Don't covet? These were harder. These needed some explaining.

Take one day a week and don't make bricks? Now that was *really* confusing.

How the Law Got Multiplied

The law explained what to do if an ox gored a neighbor. It told you what to eat and what not to eat. Let the land rest every seven years. Don't charge interest. Don't cut down a fruit tree, even in a time of war. The law protected widows, orphans, and even nesting birds.

All in all, God gave more than six hundred laws, from your obligation to your dead brother's wife to how to handle an unsolved murder. The laws seemed to cover everything, and what wasn't covered could be figured out by extension—sort of.

You see, people are people. They try to get around the law. So the rabbis started adding rules in an attempt to strengthen the law. By the time Jesus came along, there were hundreds of "derivative" sabbatical rules. Moving furniture is work. But is making the bed? How about flossing your teeth to remove a popcorn shell?

Could I, as a doctor, empty Bill's bladder on the Sabbath? Or was Bill allowed to move his bowels? Both would have been considered work. You read that right. Having a bowel movement was deemed work by some religious leaders and therefore to be abstained from for twenty-four hours each week. How can it be rest if you can't even use a restroom?

The Ten Commandments were not a curse; rather, they gave freedom to those who possessed them. They defined the borders of the Hebrew world. Within those borders there was freedom—freedom under the law. We have a tendency to circumvent the intent of good laws, resulting in more rules being added. Sabbath was meant to protect the worker and to set the stage for a celebration of God. If our day of rest becomes a set of rules, then the celebration and the joy are easily subtracted.

How the Fourth Commandment Got Subtracted

The 24/7 lifestyle is a recent development. If you have seen the movie *Chariots of Fire*, you might recall the story of Eric Liddell, a devout Christian who in 1924 was willing to give up his shot at an Olympic gold medal in order to honor the Sabbath.

During my childhood, everything still closed on

Sundays. Gas stations were closed. Pharmacies were closed.
Baseball games were called if they didn't finish before a
prescribed time so as not to encroach on the rest of the
day. We milked cows every day, but we didn't put up hay
on Sunday, even if it would get ruined. Now, factory farms
operate without relenting, as if an ancient curse had been
placed upon them.

Many factors have contributed to this change.
Electricity, computers, globalization, secularization, and
jet travel have hastened the loss of our weekly day of rest.
Expectations of students, sports, and consumerism elevated
to the level of religious fervor have only made matters
worse. And the increasing number of households with two
working parents or single parents has created a demand for
expanded hours of retail and business services.

How has this change affected us? Many books have been
written about the 1950s. By and large, these books agree
that happiness and satisfaction peaked in the late fifties and
have been on the decline ever since. Some say our collective happiness and satisfaction was a result of post–World
War II prosperity, others that we were naive and just didn't
know any better. But could it also be because society took
a break once a week from getting and spending?

One twenty-first-century irony is that the secular world
is sometimes better about keeping the intention of the
Fourth Commandment than the church is. For example,
even the most widely published atheist professor still insists
on his or her sabbatical (Sabbath leave). Judges who enforce

separation of church and state don't hold court on Sundays. Wall Street measures 24/7 profits but doesn't trade on the weekends.

For the most part, the church stands with one foot on the dock and one in the untethered boat of culture. This change leaves us with some uneasy feelings. We intuit that the Ten Commandments are a good idea, and therefore laws against killing, stealing, or bearing false witness are still on the books in every state. But the business of the church also involves laws that apply only to those who willingly submit to them: love God, don't worship idols, don't take the Lord's name in vain, remember the Sabbath, honor your mother and father.

It would be bizarre to have a pastor stand up and give a sermon proposing that we ditch these commandments. Yet many of us are effectively ripping these commandments from the pages of our Bibles. If we were truly understanding and acting upon the intent of the laws, there might be some justification for doing this, but let's not kid ourselves. We're not.

For many believers, the theology behind tossing out the Fourth Commandment is fuzzy. This is the question we must ask: Is the meaning of our lives more than making bricks, bricks, bricks—even if they are only virtual ones?

PART 2

· · · · · · · · ·

Why We Need
24/6

Work Is Sweet, for God Has Blest

Work is sweet, for God has blest
Honest work with quiet rest,
Rest below and rest above
In the mansions of His love,
When the work of life is done,
When the battle's fought and won.

Work ye, then, while yet 'tis day;
Work, ye Christians, while ye may;
Work for all that's great and good,
Working for your daily food.
Working whilst the golden hours,
Health and strength, and youth are yours.

Working not alone for gold,
Not the work that's bought and sold,
Not the work that worketh strife,
But the working of a life
Careless both of good or ill,
If ye can but do His will.

Working ere the day is gone,
Working till your work is done,
Not as traffickers at marts,
But as fitteth honest hearts,
Working till your spirits rest
With the spirits of the blest.

Godfrey Thring

CHAPTER 4

Jesus and the Sabbath

The Son of Man is Lord, even over the Sabbath.

Luke 6:5

I MISS the operating room. I miss the clear white lights and the filtered air. I miss scrubbing, gowning, and gloving; the ratcheting of a needle holder clamping down while a respirator cycles reassuringly; the surgery team absorbed in routine, oblivious to the miracles they're performing.

As much as I love the OR, though, I hold few fond memories of my surgery rotation in medical school. Back then, medical students were often mistreated and humiliated in the operating room. Once, however, I was there when the tables were turned.

An hour before the sun gave any thought to rising, I had arrived at the hospital to help harvest the saphenous vein from the leg of a patient who needed it to bypass the clogged arteries in his heart. My "helping" in this case involved dutifully daubing up behind the resident as she carefully teased out the vein.

Dr. Theodore Simpson, the surgeon who would lead the bypass team, backed through the OR door holding up his sterile, wet hands. *Whew!* I thought. *I'm sure glad it's not me assigned to Simpson today.* I'd recently been burned on the infamous Simpson grill. No senior resident, much less a student, could possibly have answered most of the questions he asked, but these interrogations were more about ego than teaching. After all, as Dr. Simpson frequently pointed out, the removal of Adam's rib is sure proof that God is a thoracic surgeon.

"There!" the resident said, bringing me back to the task at hand. She pointed her pick-up at the place that needed to be cleaned. While I finished, Dr. Simpson gloved and gowned, and the chief resident did likewise.

That's when Mike, the oldest member of our medical school class, strolled into the OR. "Good morning! How is everyone today?" Mike greeted the team, taking a towel from the scrub nurse.

It was as if someone had spit on the OR floor. By speaking distinctly and pleasantly rather than in obsequious petition, Mike had dared to elevate himself to the level of God—and by association, Dr. Simpson.

"Now that we've got a *doctor* here, we can begin," Simpson sneered.

"Great!" Mike replied. He took up a position behind Simpson and looked on.

As the heart bypass got underway, Simpson launched into his cross-examination of Mike. "Can you tell us what the first medical procedure in history was?"

Mentally, I groaned. *Here we go again.*

"People think it was thoracic surgery, because of Adam's rib," Mike answered, "but the first thing God did was cause Adam to go into a deep sleep. So the first medical procedure was actually anesthesia."

We all took a deep breath behind our masks.

"Lucky for Adam," Mike added.

Simpson seemed to ignore everything except the open chest cavity before him. But when the patient's heart was packed in crushed ice, the lead surgeon made sure that Mike was placed in the most uncomfortable position possible, with his arm bent at an awkward angle holding the freezing heart.

Timing is everything. With Mike in this compromised position, Simpson struck back: "What is the function of the nerve proximal to your hand?" To everyone's relief, Mike's answer was correct.

Dr. Simpson went on and on with his quiz, and Mike responded calmly and accurately, no matter how nitpicky the questions became. Simpson asked about obscure states of pathology. He pressed on about the lymphatic flow. As the answers kept coming, those who did not know Mike began to wonder about this masked medical student.

If in his youth Dr. Simpson had watched more *Star Wars* and dissected fewer frogs, he might have gotten a "bad feeling" about the way things were unfolding and quietly backed off. Instead, the questions got more obscure until finally they veered into the most forgettable of all medical trivia: embryology.

"What is this vessel?" asked Simpson.

"The left subclavian artery," Mike answered.

"Embryologically speaking, from which vessel does it arise?"

"An intersegmental artery," Mike replied, with the first hint of weariness at the game.

"Wrong, *doctor*! Its derivation is one of the aortic arches," Simpson corrected in smug triumph. Finally, he had won.

Mike cleared his throat and with firmness stated, "In actuality, the right subclavian artery is derived from the fourth aortic arch, whereas the left is derived from the seventh intersegmental artery."

"I suggest that you scrub out and go look it up in O'Brien's *Anatomy*. Then come back and enlighten us," Simpson countered in a tone that said Mike would never work in this town again.

With a triumphant little swagger in his knot-tying hand, Dr. Simpson returned his attention to the surgery. Mike shrugged and walked toward the OR doors. At the same time, the head of anesthesia strolled in to check on his residents.

"Professor O'Brien! You're slumming!" he said, nearly bumping into Mike.

"Just healin' the people," Mike responded. "Hey—and let Carolyn know that we still owe you a rain check on dinner. It's on us this time!"

Simpson stopped and stared dumbfounded over his magnifying loops.

"Theo, you must have been in hog heaven having Professor O'Brien scrub into your case!"

Even hidden behind a surgical mask, you can tell when someone's mouth is hanging open.

In a city with four medical schools and students rotating through forty hospitals, a surgeon can tell the author of one of the world's greatest surgical anatomy textbooks to go "look it up" without realizing it. But at some point, Simpson had probably heard the news about Mike—Professor O'Brien—quitting his teaching post in the anatomy department to enroll in medical school.

Caught up in his own power trip, Simpson had failed to recognize the true authority.

Jesus Steps Up to the Microphone

Two thousand years ago, the author of the bestselling textbook in history scrubbed into the case of all cases. Because he wore a mask of humanity, even those who had heard the rumor of his coming failed to recognize him.

On the morning in question, Jesus stood up in his

childhood church and read from the book of Isaiah: "The Spirit of the LORD is upon me, for he has anointed me to bring Good News to the poor. He has sent me to proclaim that captives will be released, that the blind will see, that the oppressed will be set free, and that the time of the LORD's favor has come" (Luke 4:18-19).

What Jesus says in his very first sermon is that *he* is the Sabbath—and not just any Sabbath. "The time of the LORD's favor" has also been translated as "the acceptable year of the Lord." What is an acceptable year of the Lord? Certainly it is much more than a single Sabbath, and even more than a month of Sundays.

The Hebrew people stopped one day a week. In addition, every seventh year was to be a special sabbatical year, one in which the land was allowed to lie fallow. Every seven cycles of seven years was followed by a year of ceasing, christened a jubilee year.

In a jubilee year, all debts are canceled, all slaves are set free, and all property reverts to its original owners. If your dad lost the farm in a Ponzi scheme, it doesn't matter—you get it back. The exiles in Babylon go home. Injustice takes a holiday. The blind have 20/20 vision. You are forgiven, redeemed, and restored.

The minute Jesus steps into his ministry, he stakes his claim on the Sabbath. Jesus declares himself both the Lord of the Sabbath (Matthew 12:8) and the meaning of the day (Luke 4:21).

To walk with Jesus through the Gospels and watch him

work is to see Sabbath restored to its original intent. On the Sabbath, he casts out demons (Mark 1:21-28; Luke 4:31-37), heals scoliosis (Luke 13:10-17), shrinks peripheral edema (Luke 14:1-6), cures blindness (John 9:1-34), feeds the hungry (Mark 2:23-28), unlocks paralysis of a hand (Matthew 12:9-14; Mark 3:1-6; Luke 6:6-11), and lowers a high fever (Mark 1:29-31; Luke 4:38-39).

The minute Jesus steps into his ministry, he stakes his claim on the Sabbath. Jesus declares himself both the Lord of the Sabbath and the meaning of the day.

The Gospel of Mark: Jesus in Action

We need go no further than the Gospel of Mark to see exactly how Jesus interacts with the Sabbath. A trip through Mark's Gospel is so action packed it can give you whiplash. It is generally agreed that Mark wrote about Jesus for a Roman audience. Romans ate fast food, cheered gladiators, and obsessively built highways. Collectively, they vacillated between high achievement and a severe case of attention deficit disorder.

As a consequence, Mark's Gospel is short and full of verbs, with no time for long forays into who begat whom. Skipping right past Mary, Joseph, and the wise men, Jesus is baptized and tempted and then rides off to round up a posse. The unkempt group gallops into Capernaum. Jesus dismounts, walks through the swinging doors of the local church, and starts performing miracles.

In the opening passages of Mark, Jesus evicts a demon from a church usher, knocks the fever out of Peter's mother-in-law, and holds a mass walk-in clinic. It is not by chance that all these miracles take place on the Sabbath. The Sabbath is all about miracles and healing. This is the kind of drama that Roman spectators could appreciate. You can almost hear the sound of a helicopter overhead as you read about the first airlifted patient in history, lowered through the roof to Jesus (Mark 2:4). And instead of sending a bill, Christ forgives the man's sins.

Before the close of Mark's second chapter, Jesus melts an IRS section chief's heart, who then throws a party people are still tweeting about. Chapter two closes with Jesus setting everybody straight on the meaning of Stop Day. It may be against the law to harvest grain on the Sabbath, but it is never wrong to feed the hungry. The laws against working were made to benefit people, not the other way around.

Chapter three of Mark opens with—you guessed it—more 24/6 guidance:

> Jesus went into the synagogue again and noticed a man with a deformed hand. Since it was the Sabbath, Jesus' enemies watched him closely. If he healed the man's hand, they planned to accuse him of working on the Sabbath.
>
> Jesus said to the man with the deformed hand, "Come and stand in front of everyone." Then he

turned to his critics and asked, "Does the law permit good deeds on the Sabbath, or is it a day for doing evil? Is this a day to save life or to destroy it?" But they wouldn't answer him.

He looked around at them angrily and was deeply saddened by their hard hearts. Then he said to the man, "Hold out your hand." So the man held out his hand, and it was restored! At once the Pharisees went away and met with the supporters of Herod to plot how to kill Jesus. (Mark 3:1-6)

This story is an instance of Jesus' enemies missing the point. They are so concerned with Jesus' unconventional way of doing things, which goes against their conception of the law, that they ignore the need for mercy in their midst. But throughout his ministry, Jesus consistently brings us to the heart of the law. When the law says not to kill, Jesus ups the ante to "don't be angry" (Matthew 5:21-22). The law says not to commit adultery, but Jesus says not to lust (Matthew 5:27-28). The law says not to covet possessions, and Jesus tells a rich young man to give everything away (Matthew 19:21).

Jesus doesn't throw out the law—he fulfills it. He is a compass pointing to the *intent* behind the law. So, if "don't kill" really means "don't get angry," then what is the intent behind "remember the Sabbath and keep it holy"? What would it look like if we upped the ante on the Sabbath?

Treated like Less than a Dog

To date, I have officiated at exactly one funeral, one wedding, and one seminary graduation. I have also made one—and only one—foray into politics.

My single legislative victory began in the ER when one of our nurses was attacked and injured by a drunken man. The police came and took the report, but they would not arrest the attacker. They said that unless they witnessed the altercation, it was not an arrestable offense; it only warranted a summons. True story.

The injury rate for ER doctors and nurses is not insignificant. And there is a reason for this: while the police and emergency room personnel both deal with the same cast of characters, only the police have guns, clubs, mace, and backup to defend them. For the most part, the ER team must deal bare handed with all the same bad actors. Nurses and ER docs have even been killed in the line of duty.

When I called the police the next day, they explained that the offense fell under the same statutes as two drunks fighting in a bar. Each had a duty to retreat. Each was assumed to be at fault. A summons was all they could issue.

I checked with other emergency departments and found that this was a problem throughout our state—and pretty much nationwide. So I enlisted the help of our local representatives to make the assault of medical personnel an arrestable crime.

Legislation was introduced, and my day in the state

capitol came. When I explained the situation before the legislative committee, they listened respectfully. Then one senator objected. "Don't we have enough laws to cover these things already?" he wanted to know. "Why should we single out medical personnel for special protection?" I explained that unlike drunks in a bar, people working on an ambulance or in a hospital cannot retreat. Back and forth it went, but I seemed unable to move this naysayer's stony heart.

Finally, I threw down my trump card: "If you bark at a police dog in this state, it is an arrestable offense." I cited the law by number. One of the legislators pulled out the code book and looked it up. There it was. "You mean that a dog has more protection than a nurse?" another asked. Even the objector knew when he was beaten. A barroom brawl is not the same as attacking a nurse on duty. The law passed in Maine and in most other states.

Chipping Away at Hardened Hearts

Jesus ran into a similar situation when he confronted a group of hard hearts:

> One Sabbath day as Jesus was teaching in a synagogue, he saw a woman who had been crippled by an evil spirit. She had been bent double for eighteen years and was unable to stand up straight. When Jesus saw her, he called her over and said,

"Dear woman, you are healed of your sickness!"
Then he touched her, and instantly she could stand
straight. How she praised God!

But the leader in charge of the synagogue was
indignant that Jesus had healed her on the Sabbath
day. "There are six days of the week for working," he
said to the crowd. "Come on those days to be healed,
not on the Sabbath."

But the Lord replied, "You hypocrites! Each of
you works on the Sabbath day! Don't you untie your
ox or your donkey from its stall on the Sabbath and
lead it out for water? This dear woman, a daughter
of Abraham, has been held in bondage by Satan for
eighteen years. Isn't it right that she be released, even
on the Sabbath?" (Luke 13:10-16)

Jesus' questions redirect our attention to what should
be obvious: A donkey gets more respect than a daughter
of Abraham? A dog has more protection than a person?
What's wrong with this picture?

Remember that the Fourth Commandment concerns
God, us, and others. God can take care of himself, but
what about the maid in Victorian England? What about
the sixty-year-old who must work at McDonald's on
Sunday? What about the illegal immigrant? And even if
humans are deserving of more respect, what about the animals that are protected under the law? Did Jesus, the "first-
born of every creature" (Colossians 1:15, KJV), come to

take away any mercy for the animals he spent his first night with? Did the "man of sorrows, acquainted with deepest grief" (Isaiah 53:3) come to add to the burdens of the poor?

Rules always have exceptions. When we put slavish adherence to rules above God's intention, we lose track of the bigger picture.

Of course, it's also possible to go too far in the other direction and ignore the commandment altogether. The early church had an on-again, off-again relationship with the Sabbath. Although observing the Sabbath is in the Top Ten that God gave to Moses, doesn't right belief matter more than right action?

> *When we put slavish adherence to rules above God's intention, we lose track of the bigger picture.*

While it is correct to assert that we are saved by grace alone, does grace nullify the *intent* of the Fourth Commandment? The church has always believed that a person can break any commandment and, through repentance and God's grace, still get to heaven. Take the name of the Lord in vain, and you might still be handed the keys of the Kingdom (Mark 14:66-72). You can steal a million and still sit next to Jesus someday. Even murder can be forgiven. But do not suppose for an instant that God was a fool for giving the commandments or that he doesn't care when we break them. He did not send his only Son so that the intent of any of the Ten Commandments, including the fourth, should be discarded.

And that's just it: the intent of the commandment—
rest—is what is important. Sabbath is meant to be a refuge,
not a prison. It protects the needy, the displaced, and the
powerless. People don't save the Sabbath; it saves us.

The meaning of rest to a man who cannot walk is to get
up and go. The meaning of rest to the hungry is food. The
meaning of rest to Peter's mother-in-law was not only to be
healed from her fever, but to offer hospitality to her son-in-
law's famous employer.

Jesus did not die on a cross so that we might ignore the
intent of the law—including the intent of Sabbath.

CHAPTER 5

More than Just Another Brick in the Wall

The things, good Lord, that we pray for,
give us the grace to labor for.

Thomas More

Work consists of whatever a body is obliged to do.

Mark Twain

WINTER IN VERMONT lasts for ten months. After winter comes mud season. That's when the state's unpaved roads turn to quicksand and suck school buses into the core of the earth. After mud season, clouds of black flies hatch and bedevil residents until fall, when the state is invaded by an equal number of tourists from Massachusetts and New York. Small wonder that Vermont is the second least populated state.

Vermont's people are taciturn. The taxes are high. And the reimbursement rate for physicians is the lowest in America. Which is why, even though we studied books, pored over maps, and racked our brains, my wife and I could think of no other place to move once I finished residency.

I am grateful we did—for it was in Vermont that I experienced my best day in medicine.

That perfect day began quietly enough when I walked into the small-town hospital to begin my twelve-hour shift. Two nurses were on duty: Sue and Bardolph. I'd worked with Sue before. Bardolph was a locum tenens from Germany, living in the States for a year while his wife lectured at a nearby college.

The department had only one patient, a ten-year-old with a sore throat and a slight fever. I peered in her ears and felt the enlarged lymph nodes in her neck. She opened her mouth and stuck out her tongue. On the back of her throat, twin pus factories gave off the characteristic odor of strep.

"Her tonsils are enlarged and infected. She's got strep throat," I said to her mother. "It's not worth running the test because I would treat her for strep even if the results came back negative."

Most moms tend to appreciate not seeing their kids gagged or having the bill run up with superfluous tests, but this girl's mother lit into me. "Not worth getting the test because we're on welfare? Afraid you wouldn't be able to make the payment on your boat?"

"Ma'am, I'll be glad to get the test, and I have no idea what insurance you have."

"Never mind," she said in a disgusted tone.

I went over to the nurse's station to dictate the note for the chart and write out a prescription. "Would you mind giving this to that girl's mother and going over the instructions?" I asked Sue.

"Oh, so you want *me* to deal with Miss Charming," she countered as she reached for the chart. We stopped and listened to the radio. The rescue squad was responding to a multicar accident with a rollover.

"Okay, I'll finish up with this girl," I said. "See if we have a surgeon making rounds, and check to see where the internist and the family doctor are." Trauma can easily overwhelm the resources of a small hospital.

I swiveled in my chair and was surprised to find myself face-to-face with my patient. "Mister," the girl whispered, "I'm sorry for the way my mom is today."

"That's okay. I'll just go over things with her, and then you can head home." I put my arm around the girl's shoulder and led her back to the exam room. A second rescue unit called in from the accident.

Mom's mood hadn't improved. She made a remark about my sloppy writing—even though I'd block printed everything except my signature. I handed over the prescription and bowed out of the room as quickly as possible. There was yet another rig calling in, this time with a man who had fallen two stories.

Bardolph was relaying whom we might be able to recruit when I felt a tug at my back. It was the ten-year-old again.

"Mister, my mom's not acting right. I think it's her sugar."

I went back to have a talk with Mom. Yes, Mom was a diabetic. No, she insisted her sugar wasn't low. Could I check? No; she accused me of wanting to run up another bill. Would she drink some orange juice? No, she hated orange juice. Would she eat something? No, she was not going to touch our lousy hospital food.

Tough situation. She wasn't a registered patient. She had not given consent to treat her, and because she was not there for herself, there was no implied consent either. Needing some evidence before running the risk of forced treatment, I asked if she could count backward from a hundred by sevens.

"One hundred, ninety-three, eighty-six, seventy-nine," she contemptuously rattled off. Tougher situation. I was stuck. A stadium full of lawyers would queue up to sue me if I treated her against her wishes. The radio continued to give reports. We were about to be inundated by trauma patients.

"Please, Mister, can you help her?" The daughter looked at me with tears in her eyes.

A pleading child tops a busload of lawyers any day. Like Jedi knights, Bardolph, Sue, and a nursing supervisor appeared unbidden. The next several moments looked more like pro wrestling than medicine. The woman fought with great strength. When we finally got a blood sugar reading, it was incompatible with life, much less the higher math and hand-to-hand combat she'd managed.

We injected glucagon and got an amp of D50 (sugar) into her. With a little fuel to run her brain, she was a new woman. She apologized and repeatedly thanked us.

From that moment on, patients flowed into the ER. By nine in the morning, the operating rooms were full. By noon, we'd filled the inpatient beds. Every off-duty nurse and every on-duty doctor was called in. Our work never bogged down; we never stopped moving. I put a hip back in place. We stabilized and transferred a man who'd exploded his neck and spine when he rolled his car. I sewed skin together like a machine. We stopped two heart attacks in their tracks. Sue and Bardolph revealed their super-powers. The family doctor on call turned out to be trained in trauma.

An hour before the shift ended, we broke the ER's record for most patients treated in a single shift. I walked home in a manic state, anxious to share the day with the one I love. That night, I slept like a teenager.

I loved working in the emergency department. I made little children feel better. People wrote me thank-you letters. Some even brought me cookies! Every couple of weeks the hospital would give me money. When someone asked me what I did, I could hold my head high and give a clear-cut answer.

But work was my identity. Now, there is certainly nothing wrong with good work, and most work *is* good work. I'm as thankful for the professionalism of someone installing brakes on my car as I am for the teachers educating our children. I don't want the cook in a restaurant to be distracted when handling perishables, nor do I want the person at the bank to misplace a decimal point. But biblically speaking, work should not define our lives.

A Lesson from Nehemiah

When someone wants to talk about building a new wing at the church, they often reach for the book of Nehemiah. Nehemiah describes one of the epic work projects in the Old Testament. If you have an old Bible in the attic that belonged to a Pilgrim, chances are the pages of Nehemiah will be heavily worn and dog-eared.

When Nehemiah arrived in Jerusalem, the city had gone to seed. The gates were missing, and the city walls lay in rubble. No one took initiative or responsibility.

But under Nehemiah's leadership, the townspeople got to work. They rebuilt the city, starting with the walls. Everyone pitched in: priests, goldsmiths, administrators, singers, and out-of-work gatekeepers.

Stones were moved, gates were built, and workers were fed. Nehemiah showed how to get people to care about what happens in their own backyard. They finished the monumental task of rebuilding the city wall in just fifty-two days.

We tend to think of city walls when we recall the book of Nehemiah, but the building part of the book occurs only in the first four chapters. And even then, many of the details of how the work was accomplished are not recorded. How did they lift the stones? Did they get the wall back up to its original height? Where did they forge the hardware for the gates? The remaining nine chapters are about what happens when God's people get beyond building the wall. The reason: Nehemiah isn't merely a treatise on work. It's about where work can take us—to prayer, repentance, feasting, living in community, and Sabbathing.

For a large part of my life, I got stuck in the first few chapters of Nehemiah. I never stopped building the wall. Only in the last decade or so have I started to understand the greatest lesson of Nehemiah: once the people finished their work, they moved on. They took stock of who they were, confessed their sins, gave away money, and studied the Scriptures. They feasted and celebrated the holidays. They sang, read more Scripture, and celebrated Sukkoth, the Festival of Booths.

> *Nehemiah isn't merely a treatise on work. It's about where work can take us—to prayer, repentance, feasting, living in community, and Sabbathing.*

The book of Nehemiah doesn't give the dimensions of a single stone used in the city's permanent wall, but it details which four species of branches the people were to use in erecting the harvest booths that would be taken down in a week. We tend to think that our work and its products are the legacy we leave. Nehemiah points toward seemingly transitory things and says they are just as permanent.

Once the stone walls of Jerusalem were rebuilt, the people concentrated on the other aspects of their relationship with God. To guard their faith, they constructed the spiritual walls and watchtower of belief—the Sabbath: "We also promise that if the people of the land should bring any merchandise or grain to be sold on the Sabbath or on any other holy day, we will refuse to buy it. Every seventh year we will let our land rest, and we will cancel all debts owed to us" (Nehemiah 10:31).

Yes, work is good, but the purpose of work is not more work. The purpose of work is to live and glorify God. One of the ways we do that best is by remembering the Sabbath and keeping it holy.

Work in the Time of Jesus

Every year Jesus' parents went to Jerusalem for the Passover festival. When Jesus was twelve years old, they attended the festival as usual. After the celebration was over, they started home to Nazareth, but Jesus stayed behind in Jerusalem. His parents didn't miss him at first, because they assumed he was among the other travelers. But when he didn't show up that evening, they started looking for him among their relatives and friends.

When they couldn't find him, they went back to Jerusalem to search for him there. Three days later they finally discovered him in the Temple, sitting among the religious teachers, listening to them and asking questions. All who heard him were amazed at his understanding and his answers.

His parents didn't know what to think. "Son," his mother said to him, "why have you done this to us? Your father and I have been frantic, searching for you everywhere."

"But why did you need to search?" he asked. "Didn't you know that I must be in my Father's house?" But they didn't understand what he meant.

Then he returned to Nazareth with them and was obedient to them. And his mother stored all these things in her heart.

Jesus grew in wisdom and in stature and in favor with God and all the people. (Luke 2:41-52)

These lines from Luke are the only mention, aside from the birth narratives, of Jesus' first thirty years of life. There is no account of high school, college, internships, or summer jobs. Did Jesus apprentice in a woodworking shop? Did he work on a commercial fishing boat? The writers of the Gospels didn't think it was important to tell us. But from this small snippet in Luke, we learn something about the priorities of the family that raised Jesus: they went to Jerusalem every year for the Passover.

Today, we would load up a vehicle in Nazareth and drive south on Route 60 to Route 65, then get on the highway at the Route 6 interchange and continue south until we hit traffic around Route 1 heading into Jerusalem. It's less than a hundred miles and takes about two hours.

. But in Jesus' time, folks had to walk—a trip of four to seven days. For every week in Jerusalem celebrating Passover, add another week and a half travel time. Career advancement clearly was not the top priority for the holy family.

We know a little about the professions of some of the disciples: four fished, one collected taxes, and one "zealoted" for a living; we know nothing about the others' occupations. And all of them quit their day jobs to follow Christ. When a crowd asked Jesus point-blank what line of work they should get into, he said, "This is the only work God wants from you: Believe in the one he has sent" (John 6:29).

It wasn't as if Jesus didn't know that people had bills to pay and kids to feed. We can tell because Jesus tended to their material needs first: he fed them, cured them, and allowed them to see. But we would be missing the point if we thought he was only interested in growling stomachs and withered limbs. He eased sorrow by raising children from the dead. He offered living water to take away thirst and the bread of life to end all hunger. He said he had come to give rest and peace.

Nowhere does the Bible encourage laziness. But neither do the Gospels record Christ handing out much career advice—other than that our most important job here on earth is to "believe."

In my early twenties, the economy was terrible, and I

had little education and no family to help me. Having no job or too little money is no picnic. I'm not advocating the life of an ascetic. But for many of us, the opposite is the rule. We have enough work, but too little time for God and life. We have enough money, but we opt for a cycle of consumption and waste. We canonize the American Dream and worship it.

We would be missing the point if we thought Jesus was only interested in growling stomachs and withered limbs. He said he had come to give rest and peace.

Today we live in one of the most prosperous eras of human history, yet many of us never get beyond survival mode. And unrelenting work can keep us from asking life's big questions: Who am I? Why am I here? What does all this mean? Jumping off the hamster wheel once a week allows us to think about who we are, why we exist, and why we were made.

The work I did as a doctor was good work. Healing the sick even has biblical precedent. But when I was a doctor, I was not a believer in God. My god was the American Dream, good work, and my kids doing well at school. In and of themselves, none of these things are bad. But none of them can replace God, either.

The key to good, meaningful work is not just to see more patients or to build more walls, but to remember why and for whom we are working.

CHAPTER 6

Resting in Rest

Be still, and know that I am God!

Psalm 46:10

ON THE LAST MORNING of fourth grade, everyone in my class was given a fountain pen. These writing instruments consisted of a plastic body—clear, blue, or red—with an ink cartridge and a metal cap. The pens represented a rite of passage: we were moving up from thick pencils and smudged newsprint with blue dotted lines down the median to three-hole-punched notebook paper and cursive writing.

During recess that day, I climbed to the top of the jungle gym, where the older boys stood upright on the thin metal pipes and extended their arms into the air. No boy below fourth grade ever attempted the "summit" trick, and although I had done it enough not to be accused of unmanliness, even I thought it was foolhardy.

Nonetheless, once I was at the top, I put my shoes on the two slippery narrow pipes, glanced at the hard surface far below, let go with my hands, and moved from a crouch to an upright position. Standing there on the roof of the world with my arms outstretched, a thought came to me. At the time, it seemed logical: *Why not do something while I'm up here?* I took out my fountain pen and decided to disassemble it. Whether from lack of oxygen or brains—or my nervousness over the precarious height—no matter how hard I pulled, I could not get the pen apart.

In desperation, I took the nib between my teeth and gave a yank. Success! The thrill of victory, however, was quickly eclipsed by the agony of swallowing a mouthful of ink while the nib, body, cap, and empty cartridge went ricocheting toward the earth. Quick as Einstein, my mind turned to the mathematical question that dogged much of the first two decades of my life: *How can I hide this?*

I was distracted from my calculations by the approach of Mary Sue Leaden. She had a quick smile, a large, freckled nose, and behind fetching glasses the most charming myopic eyes ever to grace a playground. In short, she was the most dazzling creature I could imagine. During square dancing, when other girls said, "Yuck!" she had simply taken my hand and do-si-doed. I spent countless hours daydreaming of daring ways to rescue her from peril. Always my reward for jumping in front of a bullet just in the nick of time was to die in her grateful arms.

Mary Sue looked up at me, broke into uncontrollable laughter, and ran off.

I descended from the summit and was seized at base camp by a teacher who marched me toward the school building. If you want to know what defeat tastes like, drink one teaspoon of warm alkaloid blue ink (black ink may be substituted but is not recommended), add the ridicule of the girl who matters the most to you, and then top it off with the howls of classmates or—even worse—the laughter of kids in the lower grades.

I had no illusions that they were laughing *with* me. As I walked the long path in a blur of humiliation, the teacher held me at arm's length using my ear as a handle.

"Well, Mr. Sleeth," he said, torquing my ear a few inches more from its anchoring skull, "the school is questioning whether you should be advanced to the next year." Being held back a year was the continual threat of my youth.

The teacher stood me before a mirror and asked if I thought what I saw was funny.

In front of me was a child, small for his age, sporting home-cut hair and a Goodwill shirt. He was covered with ink like a Rorschach test. His big front teeth were outlined in deep purple-indigo gums. I broke into laughter, foaming ink bubbles out my nose. Of course it was funny!

Mary Sue Leaden's family moved away that summer, and I never saw her again. My parting image of her is one of otherworldly perfection. Her last glimpse of me was as a fourth-grade madman.

That night at dinner, my father scolded me about school. I took a sip of my milk and giggled. "You think everything is a joke," he said. "You'd probably think it was funny if I dropped dead."

For a millionth of a second, I maintained control, and then I erupted in laughter. My father swatted me and sent me to my room. For the second time that day, bluish bubbles foamed out my nose.

At the beginning of each school year, the five children in my family were promised small rewards for making good grades and keeping out of trouble. I had failed on all accounts, so I was the only one not welcome on the rewards caravan that left our house in the morning.

What would have been the right punishment for breaking a new fountain pen and getting in trouble at school? It certainly wasn't leaving me out of the shopping trip, something I wasn't thrilled about anyway. Leaving me home alone was akin to punishing a child who won't eat his vegetables by making him eat ice cream.

So it was that on the first day of summer after fourth grade, in the quiet of June in farm country, I strolled across the grass toward the barn. The air was calm and soft. All worries of failure and school had vanished from the earth. It was as quiet and bright as the air above clouds.

One key element of happiness is contentment, and one of the foundations of contentment is optimism. I was happy, content, and optimistic. All of summer stretched out before me: a vast, unexplored adventure. In my arms,

I held a package my uncle had given me several weeks before. On the brown wrapping, Uncle Frank had written his instructions: "Do not open until summer vacation." My uncle had sent me the greatest of all gifts: three brand-new Hardy Boys books.

I love the writings of C. S. Lewis, Mark Helprin, Norman Maclean, Frederick Buechner, and Howard Frank Mosher. But nothing will ever compare to the supreme luxury of lying in a cool barn on that first day of vacation and reading *The Shore Road Mystery*, by Franklin W. Dixon. My misadventures with the fountain pen had led me exactly where I needed to be: a day of rest.

Everyone needs rest—not just ten-year-old boys. What do we need rest from? We need rest from being hurt, rest from our heavy labors, and rest from our fast-paced world. We need rest from the speed of change, rest from our jobs, and rest from information overload.

Rest from Being Hurt

My ignoble end of fourth grade had a happy outcome: a restful day alone. But many of life's trials don't have such a good outcome. And in some cases the consequences may stick with us for years afterward. They may be hidden or suppressed for a time, but that does not mean they are gone. Everyone picks up a collection of hurts as the years go by. Disappointment and loss are a part of life. We all hurt each other. We've all been hurt.

As an adult, I worked in the emergency department, which frequently bears witness to suffering. I cleaned up the aftermath: a child and his friend find the father's police pistol and play with it. The teacher driving home from work sneezes, reaches into her purse for a handkerchief, and doesn't see the young woman jogging. The pallet falls off the truck into the path of the teenager. Mom buckles her six-month-old into the front seat of the new van; a minor accident inflates the first-generation airbag and snaps the baby's neck. A lump is found in the breast, the testicle, or the neck.

Sometimes the hidden and secret tragedies can be even worse than the obvious ones, like the man who is faithfully married for years and finds he is HIV positive, or the children whose parents tell them one Saturday morning, "It's not your fault; Mommy and Daddy will always love you"—but not enough to stay married.

It takes time for physical tissue to recover from pain and injury. The same goes for spiritual and emotional injuries. Rest gives our souls the time they need to heal.

Rest from Heavy Labors

In addition to rest from hurts, we need rest from heavy labors. Unlike the slaves that God freed from Egypt, most of us do not struggle under heavy manual labor. Manual labor has its own reminder to stop. One can only move bricks so long before muscles cry out for rest.

Unfortunately, other types of labor may not remind us of the need to lay down our burdens. What about answering e-mails, going to meetings, and working with customers?

Move refrigerators, and your body will remind you to rest. It's obvious. But other labors demand rest as well, and it's not so obvious. When Jesus beckons us, "Come to me, all of you who are weary and carry heavy burdens, and I will give you rest" (Matthew 11:28), he calls us not just from physical burdens, but from all of life's trials.

Explaining to workaholics why they need rest is similar to explaining to alcoholics why they need sobriety, or explaining to smokers why they need to quit smoking. All are simply necessities of good health. When we rest, our blood pressure falls and levels of stress hormones such as cortisol decline. If we are to treat our bodies as temples, we must allow time for physical, mental, and spiritual recovery from the labors of our week.

> *When Jesus beckons us, "Come to me, all of you who are weary and carry heavy burdens, and I will give you rest," he calls us not just from physical burdens, but from all of life's trials.*

Rest from the Pace of the World

You have probably seen time-lapse films of people crossing intersections in New York, Tokyo, or other major cities. These sped-up scenes of crowded intersections, highways, and escalators point out the obvious by making it even more so: we live in a fast-paced world. Viewed from just a few floors above street level, our lives seem small, anonymous, and insignificant. We look like nothing more than worker ants.

In a 1990s study for the British Council, Dr. Richard Wiseman recorded how fast people walked in cities as a gauge of those cities' pace of life. Not surprisingly, faster-paced cities had higher incidences of coronary artery disease. A recent redo of Wiseman's study found that the speed of walking has increased 10 percent in cities around the globe.

Earlier in *24/6* we applied the law of science: for every action, there is an equal and opposite reaction. Speeding up our pace has an equal and opposite reaction. Fast living that includes fast food and fast eating may ultimately be slowing us down. Americans spend less than eighty minutes per day eating meals. What is the reaction? We're getting fat. Nearly 35 percent of our population has a body mass index (BMI) over 30. (A BMI of more than 25 is overweight, and one of more than 30 is considered obese.) In contrast, the French spend more than two hours a day eating, and only 10 percent of them have a BMI over 30. In 1972 Americans spent $3 billion a year on fast food; today that number is over $110 billion. By eating fast food, we get calories into our bodies *fast*, but by taking the time to cook and dine, we nourish our souls. Fast-paced lives leave less time for activities that build family and friendships. They may be so fast that they leave little time for either dining or the divine.

Taking time to sit down and eat is sacred biblical business. Abraham fed the angels under the oaks of Mamre, Jesus taught over meals in the homes of his friends, and Christ was revealed to the travelers on the road to Emmaus when they broke bread together. In the book of John, Jesus taught over a slow dinner. The meal goes on for five chapters—nearly one-quarter of the Gospel of John! Where would we be if the disciples had used the drive-thru window?

Rest from the Speed of Change

Two years ago I was on the set of a film production in the California redwoods. A tractor trailer housed a score of computers on folding tables. The computers were wired together and connected to banks of hard drives. Five young people (all under thirty—I asked) flitted between the equipment working on a technical problem. I stood in the background and marveled at their skill and competence. How wonderful it must be to belong to this generation to whom silicon-based connectivity is "intuitive"!

Then the chief computer geek typed a flurry of commands and clicked a dozen times. The problem was solved. "You know, the kids today are so much faster at these problems," he sighed. The crew murmured their agreement.

"Yeah, it's hard to keep up. I don't know what I'm going to do in ten years," another added.

If computer jocks in Hollywood, under age thirty,

wearing flannel shirts and skinny jeans with iPhones in their pockets, are worried about keeping up, what about the rest of us? What will happen when the pace of change accelerates even more?

We used to say that the letter was "in the mail." The onset of e-mail made correspondence much faster. But there was still a separation of time. After all, we couldn't be expected to carry a computer around all the time. In the early days of PCs, hardly anyone had laptops, and those who did certainly were not expected to respond to e-mail from home.

Not so anymore. My cell phone is a computer that is always connected to the Internet. It fits in my pocket; it connects by multiple networks and cell towers. If you can communicate anytime and anywhere, you can also be expected to be available 24/7. The average response time for an e-mail is ninety minutes. The average response time for a text message is ninety seconds. Today, more than 90 percent of Americans keep their mobile phones within reach 24/7.

Rest from the Job

My parents' generation tended to have long-term careers at one company, school, or profession. When I was growing up, this was the rule for both the farmers and the folks who drove off to jobs. But it is not the case for this generation, and it has not been true in my life.

I found a hospital in Maine where I loved working. I said that I would work there until the job went away. It wasn't perfect, but the doctors, nurses, and patients were first rate. After seven years, the hospital merged with another one. Our patient volume doubled, and our staffing stayed the same. We went from having a chief nurse who cared about patients to one who cared about "nursing theory." When a patient died in the department as a result of the short staffing, I knew I would have to leave or accept an unethical work situation. I left. Because experienced ER doctors are in short supply, I found another job—but not everybody has that option.

My experience of changing jobs and even professions is more the rule than the exception. It has happened to teachers, office staff, and factory workers. Uncertainty about our jobs has hit all areas of employment, and we are working more. According to the Bureau of Labor Statistics, the average young married couple in 1969 worked fifty-six hours a week. Thirty years later, this number had risen to sixty-seven hours, and it continues to accelerate. The statistics hold for couples with and without children. We work more, and we have less job certainty.

Resting is even more necessary in uncertain times. It helps us remember that God is in control and that our identity is not dependent on the work we do.

Rest from Information

Peter F. Drucker, best known for his work on management philosophy, argues that executives need large quantities of uninterrupted time to make "executive" decisions. Effective leaders carve out these blocks of time to synthesize information, weigh risks, and plan strategies. This isn't rocket science. Anthropologists tell us that leisure time made civilization possible. New advances allow more leisure time, which gives us the space to make more new advances. In medicine this is called a positive feedback loop. Positive feedback loops work well if they have an end point or reach a new steady state, but they are disastrous if left unchecked. Checks-and-balances systems tend to be more stable.

I don't know anyone who is not required to make executive decisions on a daily basis. Running a home, raising children, and just figuring out life require executive skills. Uninterrupted time allows us to separate what's important from what's merely urgent. It's all too easy to waste our lives clicking on stories of the "nine worst mistakes to make in parenting," "ten essential facts to consider before switching careers," or "four ways identity thieves fool victims."

Uninterrupted time allows us to separate what's important from what's merely urgent.

We have come a long way from one morning paper and the choice of three evening news shows. My one Internet radio service has 414 continuous-streaming news channels. Well-meaning friends forward a constant barrage of articles and clips.

Overall, US Internet users spend an average of 13 hours online each week, browsing 99 domains and 3,123 web pages. The time spent on an individual website, however, is just fifty-six seconds. In short, the river of information we see is a mile wide and a quarter of an inch deep. We need rest from the deluge of information in order to discern what information is important and how we should respond.

The Punctuation Mark of Sabbath

For me, that day alone after fourth grade is the definition of rest. We all have our own special times of stopping. The definition changes as we age and go through the different seasons of life.

Rest is stopping one's work, whatever that work may be. Rest is freedom from harassment. It is the quiet after the storm. It is children fresh out of a bath with pruned fingers and the smell of baby shampoo, tucked under their blankets before bedtime.

Rest is the sound of the night breeze rattling the palms as it comes in off the Gulf. Rest is putting your head down on the pillow knowing that you can sleep in. Rest is the beast of burden unhitched from the plow. Rest is walking around the edge of shorn cornfields in the fall. Rest is reading and setting the book aside when your eyes get too heavy. Rest is the sound of the wind through the screen porch of the beach house. Rest is stopping. It is staring up through the thin Colorado night sky at the spine of our galaxy.

Rest is thinking about all the things that you could do on a Sunday afternoon and hearing a still, small voice tell you to just stop—and then taking a God-ordained nap.

Rest is thinking about all the things that you could do on a Sunday afternoon and hearing a still, small voice tell you to just stop—and then taking a God-ordained nap.

When Moses asked God how he would convince the Israelites who had sent him, God said, "I Am Who I Am" (Exodus 3:14). In a world of constant change, God was and is and always will be; he is the Alpha and the Omega, the first and the last of all things. God is the Ancient of Days and the new day's Bright Morning Star. In short, God is timeless.

Life knocks us around. We carry childhood humiliations and deep, adult aches. These injuries happen directly, of course, but when we love, we also share the pain of others. We take on a whole new set of burdens; occasionally we hurt others and they hurt us.

Physical bruises heal, and mental ones can as well—but it takes time. True rest cannot be purchased. It is not instantaneous. It is glimpsed out of the corner of the eye through the window of faith. It lies in a land apart. It is felt in contrast to the things it is not. Rest is enjoyed through the perspective of honest work.

Jesus calls out to us in this 24/7 world of constant change and says, "Let me teach you, because I am humble and gentle at heart, and you will find rest for your souls.

For my yoke is easy to bear, and the burden I give you is light" (Matthew 11:29-30). In learning how to rest, we actually gain knowledge of Christ. We learn to be gentle and humble and to give up our pride.

For many years my wife, Nancy, taught English. On the first day of class, she asked students to write an essay. She wanted to assess their writing skills and get to know them better. One semester she showed me an essay from Clinton. Clinton's essay was three pages long. It did not contain a single comma, semicolon, period, or paragraph indentation. It was one long, run-on sentence.

God did not intend our lives to be like Clinton's paper, a continuous run-on sentence. Musicians say that it is not the notes but the pauses between the notes that make music. To add meaning to our lives, God gave us the punctuation mark of the Sabbath.

My ideal day of rest may no longer revolve around a Hardy Boys book, but it is most certainly quiet. It is a day when I trust that the world can get along just fine without Matthew.

PART 3

How We Do 24/6

Abide with Me

Abide with me; fast falls the eventide;
The darkness deepens; Lord with me abide.
When other helpers fail and comforts flee,
Help of the helpless, O abide with me.

Swift to its close ebbs out life's little day;
Earth's joys grow dim; its glories pass away;
Change and decay in all around I see;
O Thou who changest not, abide with me.

Hold Thou Thy cross before my closing eyes;
Shine through the gloom and point me to the skies.
Heaven's morning breaks, and earth's vain shadows flee;
In life, in death, O Lord, abide with me.

Henry F. Lyte

CHAPTER 7

It's about Time

I lavish unfailing love for a thousand generations on
those who love me and obey my commands.

Exodus 20:6 (from the second of the Ten Commandments)

I MET NAOMI on a Tuesday evening. Her mother drove
her straight from the high school. Naomi had been at field
hockey practice when her left arm and shoulder started
hurting—again. She sat on a stretcher, a sixteen-year-old
somewhat out of place in the main bay of our department.

I love the unspoken language that passes between parents and children who care about one another. Like the
pull of heavy rare-earth magnets, yet stronger and softer, it
always draws them closer. Naomi radiated wholesomeness
and youth.

Her mother told me that Naomi had started experi-
encing pain in her left arm at the beginning of the school

year. Maybe it was worse with activity; it was hard to tell. She had seen a nurse-practitioner and been advised to use ibuprofen three times a day. Maybe that helped, but the pain came back. They saw the nurse-practitioner two more times and were referred to a physical therapist.

Was the therapy helping? No. Had they gotten an X-ray? No. Had the pain ever woken Naomi from sleep? Yes. Any cough? No. Night sweats? No. Weight loss? No.

"She hurt so much when she was at practice today, she was almost in tears," her mother said as I pushed on Naomi's shoulder. Yet there was no pain with palpating or putting the shoulder through the range of motion. Naomi seemed embarrassed by the lack of symptoms, like when the strange noise in my car cannot be reproduced in front of the mechanic. But I believed every word.

I took the stethoscope slung around my neck and placed the diaphragm on Naomi's back. Listening as hard as I could, I heard nothing wrong. The lung fields on the left matched those on the right. Her face was symmetrical, and there was no drooping eyelid. Still, my stomach fell away. Everything about this case felt wrong. "Let's get a chest X-ray," I suggested. Maybe my facial mask wasn't as impenetrable as I had thought: they didn't ask why I was x-raying the chest instead of her shoulder.

I saw a few other patients while Naomi was getting her X-ray, then put the film up to view. In the left upper lobe of her lung sat an ugly, softball-size tumor.

Naomi died a few months after I met her. She had less

life than the threescore and ten years the Bible allots. What did she do in those final days? What does anyone do who has only a year, a month, or a day left?

If they live until they are eighty, Naomi's parents will think about her every single day. Although the pain will lessen over time, it will never go away. They will grow old, but she will be forever young. Each year, they become more convinced that Alfred, Lord Tennyson, was right about having loved and lost.

This is a book about the Sabbath, and the Sabbath and the Fourth Commandment are about time. Unlike many other religious systems, the Judeo-Christian one is intimately concerned with time. We do not believe that the clock of the universe forever resets itself. We believe there was a beginning, and there will be an end. Time is valuable.

One Day Equals One Week and Other Time Paradoxes

The Bible has always told us that time is relative, but it wasn't until Albert Einstein and George Hubble came along that we had the scientific evidence to confirm it. Throughout most of history, we had no framework to show that time changes when viewed through different lenses, but this truth has been evident since the first book of the Bible.

Two thousand years ago, Jesus said, "I come quickly" (Revelation 22:20, KJV). Two thousand years ago! What did he mean? If Jesus will be back in a flash, then what were

Gabriel and Mary talking about? When Gabriel foretold
the birth of John the Baptist, he said John would "turn
the hearts of the fathers to their children" (Luke 1:17),
meaning that the current generation would stop thinking
so much about itself. Three times in the Magnificat (Luke
1:46-55) Mary refers to God's blessings flowing from generation to generation. In this, she echoes the warning and
the promise in the Ten Commandments. Children, grandchildren, and great-grandchildren pay for their parents'
hatred of the Lord, but the Lord says, "I lavish unfailing
love for a thousand generations on those who love me and
obey my commands" (Exodus 20:6). How can we have a
thousand generations and close the show up tomorrow?

Genesis opens with the heavens and the earth being
made in seven days. Genesis 2:4 says, "These are the *generations* of the heavens and the earth when they were created, in the *day* that the LORD God made the earth and the
heavens" (ESV, italics mine). This paradox is written into
the Hebrew Bible, the King James Version, and the English
Standard Version, though some of the Bibles on my shelf
have worded it differently because the translators could not
get their minds around it. (Bible translators don't always
keep up with physics.) Rabbinical scholars of old have
struggled with this paradox for centuries. Seven days, generations, a day: which is it?

Such literary paradoxes are intentionally used by the
author of Genesis (God) to shake readers (us humans) by
the shoulders and make a point. In Genesis 2:4, the point

is not a day, a generation, or a week. The point is that God is the inventor of time. He is the author of life, the universe, and eternity. But God is not bound by time as we are.

Thinking More like a Child

When we are young, we don't know what day it is. We don't know where we are or where we're going. We live attuned to the ticking of our stomachs and dream the secret dreams of babies. We listen to lullabies and the rhythmic sounds of cars. We hear the birds others are too busy to notice. Time seems endless. Eternity stretches between birthdays. Are we there yet?

When Jesus said we have to become like children to enter the Kingdom of Heaven, was he referring to a child's sense of time? Was he pointing us to that period of our lives when we could live in the moment? Was he referring to the wonderment that allowed us to notice the moon in the middle of the day? How long has it been since you were fascinated by your shadow? It mesmerized you the first time you noticed it, yet you probably pay it no mind now. Did it lose its wonder, or did you lose your wonderment? And if you can't even see your shadow, how are you going to see God working in your life?

Jesus tells us to "take no thought" for what we wear, eat, or drink (Matthew 6:25, KJV). How do we reconcile that with planning for our children's college educations?

How in good faith can we follow a homeless Savior and sign a thirty-year mortgage? How do we "take no thought" for what we eat but believe that "those who won't care for their relatives, especially those in their own household, have denied the true faith . . . [and] are worse than unbelievers"(1 Timothy 5:8)?

The Bible is not for simpletons. Those who try to make it so risk taking the faith away from those who actively engage their brains. Likewise, those who dissect, parse, and study the Bible to death can kill the faith of children; it would be better for them to throw themselves in a lake with a stone around their necks.

Finding a Reference Point to Make It Clear

Let's make sense of Jesus telling us that he will come soon *and* Gabriel, Mary, and God telling us to think long term. Let's find the ground between giving no thought to what we eat and planting trees for our grandchildren.

In order to do this, we must get a handle on time. There is no better place to start than Psalm 90, a song attributed to Moses. Like most of the Psalms, it has a key phrase, a takeaway point to remember if you recall nothing else. Because the Psalms can lose much in modern translations, I give you the modern New Living Translation for clarity's sake side by side with the King James Version for poetry's sake. Choose one and write it on the fleshy tablet of your heart:

Psalm 90
NEW LIVING TRANSLATION

Lord, through all the
generations
you have been our home!
Before the mountains were
born,
before you gave birth to the
earth and the world,
from beginning to end, you
are God.

You turn people back to dust,
saying,
"Return to dust, you
mortals!"
For you, a thousand years are
as a passing day,
as brief as a few night
hours.
You sweep people away like
dreams that disappear.
They are like grass that
springs up in the
morning.
In the morning it blooms and
flourishes,
but by evening it is dry and
withered.
We wither beneath your anger;
we are overwhelmed by
your fury.
You spread out our sins before
you—
our secret sins—and you
see them all.
We live our lives beneath your
wrath,

Psalm 90
KING JAMES VERSION

Lord, thou hast been our
dwelling place in all
generations.
Before the mountains were
brought forth, or ever
thou hadst formed the
earth and the world,
even from everlasting
to everlasting, thou art
God.
Thou turnest man to
destruction; and sayest,
Return, ye children of
men.
For a thousand years in thy
sight are but as yesterday
when it is past, and as a
watch in the night.
Thou carriest them away as
with a flood; they are as
a sleep: in the morning
they are like grass which
groweth up.
In the morning it flourisheth,
and groweth up; in the
evening it is cut down,
and withereth.
For we are consumed by thine
anger, and by thy wrath
are we troubled.
Thou hast set our iniquities
before thee, our secret
sins in the light of thy
countenance.
For all our days are passed
away in thy wrath: we

ending our years with a
groan.

Seventy years are given to us!
Some even live to eighty.
But even the best years are
filled with pain and
trouble;
soon they disappear, and we
fly away.
Who can comprehend the
power of your anger?
Your wrath is as awesome as
the fear you deserve.
Teach us to realize the brevity
of life,
so that we may grow in
wisdom.

O Lord, come back to us!
How long will you delay?
Take pity on your servants!
Satisfy us each morning with
your unfailing love,
so we may sing for joy to
the end of our lives.
Give us gladness in proportion
to our former misery!
Replace the evil years with
good.
Let us, your servants, see you
work again;
let our children see your
glory.
And may the Lord our God
show us his approval
and make our efforts
successful.
Yes, make our efforts
successful!

spend our years as a tale
that is told.
The days of our years are
threescore years and
ten; and if by reason
of strength they be
fourscore years, yet is
their strength labour and
sorrow; for it is soon cut
off, and we fly away.
Who knoweth the power
of thine anger? even
according to thy fear, so
is thy wrath.
So teach us to number our
days, that we may apply
our hearts unto wisdom.
Return, O Lord, how long?
and let it repent thee
concerning thy servants.
O satisfy us early with thy
mercy; that we may
rejoice and be glad all
our days.
Make us glad according to
the days wherein thou
hast afflicted us, and the
years wherein we have
seen evil.
Let thy work appear unto thy
servants, and thy glory
unto their children.
And let the beauty of the
Lord our God be upon
us: and establish thou
the work of our hands
upon us; yea, the work
of our hands establish
thou it.

For many, the most memorable phrase is line twelve: "Teach us to realize the brevity of life, so that we may grow in wisdom" (NLT)/"Teach us to number our days, that we may apply our hearts unto wisdom" (KJV).

Foolish people are the ones who act like the ride never stops. They do not take the time to contemplate the limitation of "threescore years and ten." They think they will get out of this life alive. For them, Jesus does come quickly. No one's personal end time is far off.

This psalm opens with a reminder: God is in business for eternity. He has always been and always will be, and if we want to know him better, we had better develop a perspective that sees beyond our short horizon. We serve a God with more than a five-year plan. In order to resonate with the eternal character of God, we need to roll up our sleeves and get to work fixing up the place.

God is in business for eternity. He has always been and always will be, and if we want to know him better, we had better develop a perspective that sees beyond our short horizon.

This psalm asks God to renew joy and faith each morning. It does not ask God to banish all pain and suffering; instead, it seeks a balance. Give us gladness in proportion to the hard times, it says. There are seasons in life. There are rhythms to be lived. It does not dish out a saccharine-sweet faith from a church entertainer illustrating five easy steps to spiritual riches. Instead, Psalm 90 beseeches us to see the Lord's hand at work throughout every day, month, and year of our lives.

Teach Us to Number Our Days

It stands to reason that the devil is not happy about the Fourth Commandment. His object is to rid the world of all the Ten Commandments, starting with the top ones.

When the French revolted in 1789, they attempted to throw out God and king. The king lives in the palace—off with his head. God dwells in the Sabbath—get rid of the seven-day week. For a dozen years, the French adopted a ten-day week. It failed, along with the French Revolution.

In 1929, the Russians revolted against God and czar. Instead of adopting the French ten-day week, they switched to five-day workweeks. Their efforts to throw out the Sabbath also failed.

A new tactic is being employed today. It is called 24/7.

I started life with Sabbath. In the home I grew up in, we went to church on Sundays, but by the time I was in my twenties, I had sworn off sentimental and superstitious things like God. I met Nancy when she was eighteen. She was from a Jewish family. They lit candles on Friday evenings—a traditional way of welcoming the Sabbath—but her practice did not extend beyond reciting a few Hebrew blessings and sharing a family meal.

We married against our parents' wishes. I went to college and then medical school. We had children. We pursued the state religion of success. We were good at it, and we climbed up rungs of the ladder. We built a nice home. We made and saved money.

Our children grew up with all the holidays and none of the pesky problems associated with genuine faith—things like surrender, service, and sacrifice. They seemed to cope with the amalgamation and confusion. At Christmastime, they thought that the Fiddler on the Roof slid down the chimney, and if he saw his shadow, he left Hanukkah candy beside the carrots we'd left out for the reindeer.

More than a decade into my career, I started working at a hospital where they put me in charge. Not wanting to take advantage of my position, I gave the scheduling duties to another doctor. She signed me up to work every Sunday for a year while she took every Sunday off. She somehow reasoned that since she and her husband didn't have children and I did, I couldn't possibly mind.

That time of life was difficult. It was filled with loss and tragedy. I realized for the first time that there was evil afoot in the world. To quote Dante, "In the middle of the journey of our life I came to my senses in a dark forest, for I had lost the straight path."

Because of my work schedule, I began taking every Saturday off. This wasn't for any spiritual reason, but merely to shepherd strength for the next day's twenty-four-hour shift. I decided not to go shopping or do projects around the house and instead took walks, read, and rested. I also sought answers in new places. Most of the books I had read were silent on the subjects of good and evil, so I began investigating the world's great sacred texts, starting with the Hindu epics—the *Ramayana* and the *Bhagavad Gita*.

Then one slow Sunday afternoon at the hospital, I spotted a Bible on a waiting room table. I picked it up. I had never read it, and we didn't have one at home. So I stole it.

I studied the New Testament and encountered Jesus. My life has never been the same.

I tell this story not to illustrate my conversion to Christianity, but to show what can happen when someone stops working one day a week—and goes knocking on the doors of faith. "Seek, and you will find," says Jesus (Matthew 7:7, ESV). But one must first have the time to seek.

I believe that God gave the Fourth Commandment so that we could grapple with the number of our days. When I slowed to a stop, I became intensely curious about what happens—spiritually, not just physically—when someone dies. I wanted to know if life mattered. I began to number my days.

Rest, Renewal, and Reverence

How does one balance a world formed in seven days, generations, and a week? My experience has shown that this happens best on the Sabbath. Believers of old said that if everyone kept the Sabbath, time itself would cease. The river of time would freeze, and we would see God.

My Saturday "Stop Days" launched me on a journey toward the three Rs of Sabbath: rest, renewal, and reverence. In Sabbath keeping, we rest from more than our labors. We rest from the tyranny of the urgent, the staggering precipice of eternity, and the mundane workweek.

In the Sabbath's renewal, we catch a glimpse of the divine. And our response to the divine is reverence.

Rest, renewal, and reverence all take time. And if time is money, then how much time will a lifetime of Sabbath keeping cost? In what turns out to be another paradox, it may not cost anything. Sabbath keeping may be free, and it's been scientifically studied.

In *The Blue Zones*, author Dan Buettner looked for groups around the world who lived longer and healthier lives. The groups he identified lived about a dozen years longer on average than the general population. All the groups did the kinds of things you'd expect. They didn't smoke or eat a diet high in animal fat. They walked a lot. They valued family and relationships.

Life is unpredictable. We should always be at peace with God. Observing a Sabbath ensures that at the very worst, we are never more than six days away from a holy perspective.

In the United States, the community that met Buettner's criteria was in Loma Linda, California—the Seventh-day Adventists. Adventists are Sabbath keepers. On average, the cohort in Loma Linda lives about a dozen years longer than the rest of America. If you multiply the number of

Sabbaths they observe per year by their average lifespan and divide that figure by 365, you will end up with about a dozen years. In other words, the number of extra years they live is roughly equivalent to the number of days they spend in Sabbath keeping. It may be coincidence, but the Bible hints at a cause-and-effect relationship between keeping the Sabbath and living a long life. Living 24/7 is life draining; living 24/6 is life giving.

Teach us to number our days. As Naomi's story illustrates, life is unpredictable. We should always be at peace with God. The cares of the world want to drag us away from that peace. Observing a Sabbath ensures that at the very worst, we are never more than six days away from a holy perspective. Sabbath keeping gives us the time to set priorities—for a day, for a week, and for generations.

CHAPTER 8

A Sense of Place

Take off your sandals, for you are standing on holy ground.

Exodus 3:5

I USED TO LOVE watching films in the darkened class-rooms of our elementary school. A movie was a welcome break from reading, writing, and spending yet another day failing to master the basics. My attention span was shorter than an eyelash, but films about volcanoes, Eskimos, or "our friend the atom" held me entranced.

Year after year, my teachers struggled, but things like the long and short of division didn't seem to fit into my brain. All the tools of modern education were employed—everything from extinction techniques to operant learn-ing—but they failed. When the standard techniques weren't successful, they switched to theoretical and experimental teaching methods. They tried positively reinforcing me with stickers and negatively conditioning me with lost privileges, but I was the most frustrating pupil in the room.

There was only one time when I excelled. My moment came when the lights were dimmed, the curtain was drawn, and the film projector was turned on. Mrs. Hawkins's nicotine-stained hand rotated the projector's switch toward play, and if the picture shook or if the narrator's voice came out like a chorus of gargling frogs—that was my moment! I might never conquer the multiplication tables, but I understood to thread a film projector.

Mrs. Hawkins would turn off the projector and fiddle with it for a time. One of the other students might giggle or whisper, but for once our teacher knew it wasn't my fault. With a mixture of frustration and resignation, she would turn toward me and bark, "Well, Matthew, you might as well get over here and fix this thing."

One film—*The Face of Lincoln*—has retained a place in my memory. This twenty-minute, black-and-white documentary features an art professor from UCLA. He looks like a corporate man—bald and wearing a starched shirt and tie, and also a long smock. Made without the aid of color, computers, or a single special effect, the film features no props or flashy scenery. Its cast consists solely of the straitlaced professor and ten pounds of clay.

Using his fingers, a few basic tools, and a massive amount of talent, he molds a lump of clay into a lifelike bust of Abraham Lincoln. While his hands shape the likeness, his voice molds the minds of his young viewers.

Over half a century has passed since the film was first produced (and won an Academy Award for best short film), yet revisiting the film online recently, I found the message as engaging as ever. It helped me visualize a part of the Bible that has never quite made sense to me.

Genesis describes God forming Adam out of the earth: "The LORD God formed man of the dust of the ground, and breathed into his nostrils the breath of life; and man became a living soul" (Genesis 2:7, KJV). Until recently, this description did not bring any plausible imagery to my mind. Watching Professor Gage form the bust of Lincoln lifted the veil and illuminated the shortcomings of my imagination: God is not only a potter; he is a sculptor.

The word *Adam* is derived from the Hebrew word for the ground, dirt, earth, clay. God sculpts the ground and blows the breath of life into it. Despite all our cell membranes, electron transport chains, and protein enzymes, we are still inexorably a part of the earth.

Ungrounded and Uprooted

We have a long tradition of biblical and modern language alluding to our connection with the earth. For example, Jesus used clay to heal the sight of a blind man (see John 9:6-7). Today, a well-balanced person is said to be "grounded." Gage described young Lincoln as a man with "the smell of the soil" clinging to him. Yet despite our biblical heritage and our admiration for Abraham Lincoln and other ancestors who tilled the earth, we are a distinctly ungrounded generation.

One problem is that we have no roots. The average American moves every seven years. My family is less grounded than most. We have moved again and again. We moved as newlyweds to begin college, then again for medical school. We moved for residency and then for my first job, which lasted less than a year. For a dozen years we settled on the coast of Maine, which is the place my children call home. When Clark and Emma started college, we all moved to Kentucky. Looked at individually, each move was for something undeniably good. The last was to follow a call from the Lord: who can argue with that? But I miss the years in one place with the kids, just as I miss being grounded in the Maryland farmscape of my youth.

Even today, nearly forty years after I left home, I can still smell the complicated fragrance of hay and the simple smell of straw. I know the scent of molasses and grain in a wooden feed box. I yearn to know again which way the streams flow and which direction the birds will fly in the fall. I ache to be back in the barn during the snowstorm that kept us out of school for a week. Home for me and many others has become an elusive longing.

I hear this longing every time someone tells me about connecting on Facebook with an old friend from school. How close was the old friend if you haven't touched base for the past twenty years? Perhaps what we long for is not so much the person but the place. We are searching for a connection to home.

A Wandering Generation

Today's generation wanders like Hebrews in the desert. We want to go back in time, but we can't. Most of the fields behind our childhood homes have been planted with roads and strip malls. Because we don't know how to go forward, we long to go back.

We are a hydroponic society, fed by the drip irrigation of electronic social networks. These networks are not all bad. They keep us in touch with family and friends no matter where we are on the globe. But there is nothing like being with the ones you love in physical time and space.

Our wandering generation is not nomadic in the same way as those who graze the steppes of Mongolia or follow herds of arctic caribou. Unlike them, we don't know what constellation will rise in the spring. We have no idea when the thrush will push the fledgling out of the nest. We don't know what is native and what is invasive. We live in mobile homes that aren't mobile and move from our "permanent" addresses.

The Sabbath commandment tells us to remember. Remember that you are made in the image of the divine. Do not forget!

At the center of our constant shifting and moving is an ache to be back in God's presence. The Sabbath commandment tells us to remember. *Remember* that you are made in the image of the divine. Do not forget! Tie a string around your finger. Write "God" on your forehead with a ballpoint pen. Make time once a week for the process of remembering. Don't forget to stop. Meet God in time *and* space. Remember the Sabbath—to keep it holy.

Grounded in the Sabbath

The word *holy* first occurs in the second chapter of Genesis. The seventh day is blessed as holy because the Lord stopped and rested. Stopping and resting are the working definitions of holy. We are introduced to the creative aspects of God through the making of the heavens and the earth, but we learn about other qualities of God through the concepts of rest and stopping. These two concepts are not the same. Rest is done by stopping. By coming to a stop, we give rest a place to happen. We make rest possible.

But instead of resting, we move and move and don't stop to know what we are walking on. We are ungrounded. No place means much of anything to us. When no place is our home, then the whole earth is reduced to a commodity. The most we can be is consumers.

The Sabbath commandments contained in the Old Testament set the worth of all things. The ground is allowed to rest every seventh year. The newborn calf cannot be taken immediately from its mother. The fruit tree has a right to exist in a time of war.

I do not advocate the throwing over of civil law in favor of Old Testament law, but I do believe in the inherent worth that God places in his creation. Often we see no worth in what the Lord created beyond its utilitarian value. We talk about forests as timber and flowers as bouquets. Yet when God placed the trees on the earth, he said that they were pleasing to the eye (Genesis 2:9). He dresses the lilies of the field more lavishly than a king (Matthew 6:28-29). God's soliloquy to Job is about the mystery and beauty that creation has beyond its usefulness to humanity. When we take Paul's words to the Colossians to heart—"Everything was created through him and for him. He existed before anything else, and he holds all creation together" (Colossians 1:16-17)—we realize that the very ground we walk on and the air we breathe are the constant outpouring of God's creativity and love.

Stepping onto Holy Ground

When it comes to practicing what I preach about taking a day of rest, I do. Not so with staying put. In general, it is a good idea to take advice from people who have been successful at what they are talking about. There are too many marriage counselors who are working on their third or fourth marriages. But in the case of being ungrounded,

I am guilty as charged. I am no Wendell Berry. My authority on place is not derived from a lifetime of tilling beside the Kentucky River. Like most Americans, I have lost my childhood home, and I can't go back. It no longer exists.

But there are occasions when we can learn from the person who has gotten it all wrong. I have been as uprooted as an astronaut, and it is not good. And so as one who has been adrift and ungrounded, I give this advice: get grounded.

A Sabbath day is a good day to stay at home if you are always on the go. Step onto holy ground. Get to know the area around you. You do not need to get in a car and travel to the rim of a canyon or the top of a mountain. In fact, you shouldn't. Sit on the back stoop. That is where the rabbit in my yard can be seen. The world seems a little saner when he turns to stare at me and the evening sun lights up the blood vessels in his ears. There is wonder lurking at the back door of many homes. When was the last time you came upon a turtle in the yard? Are they missing, or are you not seeing them because you haven't looked? The answer matters.

In Jesus' time, there was a rule about how far one could walk on a Sabbath. The distance is thought to be about two-thirds of a mile. Walking a leisurely three miles an hour, one got to the end of one's rope in a scant dozen or so minutes. There is a great deal to be found inside the circumference of such a world. It is the size of a child's world, which means it is much larger than the one most adults know intimately. The Sabbath day's journey invites us to expand our horizon.

Maybe the rabbis of old got something right with those distance rules. Though we are no longer bound by the law, on our day of rest it may be a good practice to explore the world close by. We spend so much time whizzing around in cars that it might be restful to reconnect with the places we live.

In Jesus' time, there was a rule about how far one could walk on a Sabbath. Walking a leisurely three miles an hour, one got to the end of one's rope in a scant dozen or so minutes.

I am fascinated by the spaces close to people's houses that go unexplored. One way to find them is to follow the water. The streams in many towns are largely forgotten. They can pass under our roads without notice. You do not need to plan an exotic getaway; just walk somewhere you haven't been before. Within a few blocks of me, there is a sinkhole filled with water, and there is a stream that runs in the rainy season. There is a giant Osage orange tree. They are there for the looking.

You may not live in a dramatic landscape with romantic vistas, but the space right around you needs someone who sees the sparrows fly or fall from the sky. This may be the intent behind the keeping of Sabbath. When we shut the lawn mowers off, we find that the birds have been singing. And the Lord is known to use an even quieter voice.

Stopping and staying in place yields the kind of stillness that allows us to hear and see what has always been there. Let the Lord form you where you are. Give him the space to blow the breath of life into you, wherever he has grounded you.

CHAPTER 9

Maggots in the Manna

How long will these people refuse to obey my
commands and instructions? They must realize
that the Sabbath is the LORD's gift to you.

Exodus 16:28-29

FOR OVER A DECADE, I practiced medicine on Maine's
three-thousand-mile granite coast. It is not a place where
the land gently yields to the sea. The state's 4,600 islands
act as a vanguard in a never-ending struggle, while the
ocean advances in tides so huge that mighty rivers such as
the Kennebec regularly run backward in retreat. Men and
women who venture out in the Gulf of Maine to earn their
living do not frequent the emergency department with
frivolous complaints.

Next time you sit down to dine on lobster, understand
why the price is dear. Much effort goes into getting the
crustacean from the cold ocean floor to the warm butter on

your tabletop. The process begins by retrieving a brightly painted buoy and pulling traps up hand over hand, or in the case of the professionals, throwing the line on the take-up reel of a power winch.

Once the traps are hauled in, legal-sized lobsters are banded; little ones and egg-laying females are tossed back along with the opportunistic crabs. The trap must then be rebaited with herring to start the cycle over.

Todd Dowell lobstered for a living. One Saturday morning, he and his stern men were pulling the last traps of the week. When Todd threw the line on the winch, he hesitated for a moment. Maybe it was his left brain multiplying pounds of lobster in the keeper bin times the going rate. Maybe it was his right brain dividing what could be done on his day off. Who knows? Whatever the reason, he didn't pull his hand away quickly enough, and the winch took off the little, ring, and middle fingers—wedding band and all. Gone: just like that. And he was left-handed.

"Well, let's get a look at it," I said to Todd in the emergency room as I positioned his left hand on an operating armboard and began unwrapping the soaked towel. For many years, I passed out at the sight of blood, an aversion I overcame in the third year of medical school. Dealing with blood and guts is still not something that comes naturally to me. But unwrapping a wound and not flinching is an important part of an ER doc's job. In not reacting, in talking calmly, one is saying, "Despite this missing limb or deformity, you are still human and worthy of love and respect."

I checked the extensor and the flexor tendons, then put on magnifying loops and looked for bits of glove amongst the gristle and pulp. "We'll need to have the hand surgeon close a flap over the missing fingers," I said. "But the good news is that the index finger and the thumb are 100 percent. You'll still be able to do most of what you could do before."

"I thought so when we pulled the rest of the traps," he commented.

"You mean you worked after you lost the fingers?" I asked, amazed.

He nodded. "Yup, only had about forty-five minutes of work left," he said in the characteristic down-eastern tone. Pulling traps for almost an hour with three fingers ripped off? No wonder they call them Maineiacs! Todd was tough—or stubborn, depending on your point of view.

On the Shore of a Brave New World

More than once I have driven along while adjusting the radio or daydreaming and realized that miles have gone by while my attention was focused elsewhere. Exhausted from long ER shifts, I have even dozed for a moment on the ride home. We all do things like that sometimes. Mostly we get lucky. We drift, and because we are going in the right direction, we catch ourselves in time.

In general, however, one can no longer head home, fall asleep, and assume that "the horse knows the way to carry the sleigh." We live in a mechanized environment. The second hand on my watch goes around once a minute, but in the same amount of time, a text message going at the speed of light travels 11.2 million miles. We have passed the jet age like it was sitting still. If we drift off for a moment, something can go terribly wrong; we don't have to be operating power equipment for disasters to occur.

Humanity has waded into a shoreline between real and virtual, between solid and fluid. What is real, and what is make-believe? What is 3-D, and what has four dimensions?

My children were raised with technologies and possibilities that didn't exist when I was young. I was in no particular rush to help them get ahead in that world. I grew up on science fiction in the 1960s, where the HAL 9000 computer seemed as much warning as it was entertainment.

The first computer in our home was one a neighbor had given my kids. It came with a game called The Oregon Trail. The object of The Oregon Trail was to teach school-age children about getting from east to west in the 1800s. In the game you could load up supplies and choose your profession. Your party could stop and hunt when needed. The computer told you when you drowned in a river and when someone died of snakebite. It let you know if one of your children had "wandered off," never to be seen again. You could take along a Bible, although two hundred pounds of bear meat seemed to get you farther. I worried

about my kids spending any time at all on the computer—
and where it was all going. But for the most part, they
preferred playing in the real world, so how worried should
I be? If they died on the Oregon Trail, all they needed to
do was hit "replay." Those were the stakes of the computer
world back then. So I watched from the sidelines.

The virtual world is abstract no longer. Soldiers sip
coffee while watching through the robotic eyes of killing
drones in far-off places. A slip of the finger, a momentary
loss of concentration, press "send," and off goes a missile or
a missive. Who is in the crosshairs? What's in the address
bar? Is a thread attached? Who got copied?

A friend of ours lost her job over an e-mail attachment.
It has been two years, and she is still out of work. "Virtual"
mistakes have cost more than one job, marriage, or friendship. We have learned that the virtual and the analog are
linked in the real world. The connection between the two
has never been more real. Cyber bullying, online affairs,
and identity theft aren't virtual; they are real. There is not
one of the Ten Commandments that cannot be broken
with an iPad.

The argument about what's real and what's virtual is as
old as Plato and Aristotle. I bring up this discussion of real
and virtual because we've been taught in school that one
or the other is what matters. But the Bible says both do.
Both the physical and spiritual are important. Jesus is forever telling his listeners about the connection between the

two. Christ is the link between refreshing waters and Living Water, between filling bread and the Bread of Life.

As heirs to the Pilgrims, we tend to place great value on work and its by-products. Because of that, we believe that rest is less noble than work. "A stitch in time saves nine," "a penny saved is a penny earned," and "idle hands are the devil's playground" are just some of the sayings that extol the value of thrift and work. I come up short, however, when I search my memory for aphorisms about quiet, meditation, and prayer.

The Bible commends industry and work, but it also warns of their getting in the way of spiritual vision. Jesus sounds the alarm about missing the boat in the parable of the great feast (Luke 14:15-23). People are invited to the wedding banquet—the Kingdom of Heaven. But two of the invitees give work-related excuses for not accepting the invitation: one says he must attend to a real estate deal, and another gives the excuse of needing to mow the grass.

Sabbath keeping is nothing less than grabbing onto the robe of the Maker of the universe.

It took awhile for me to feel as good about resting on Sabbath as coming home from a productive day at work. Work seemed more real. The hospital gave me money for working. I could buy things with money. Not so for a day of rest. But I was accounting in earthly terms. I was not taking Christ's advice on laying up treasures in heaven.

For me, Sabbath has become a very real and powerful day of the week. My busy workweek is balanced by a rest day. Some books about the Sabbath extol the day's healing powers, and there are those who tout its refreshing virtues. It's true: the Sabbath was meant to restore and renew our souls. But Sabbath keeping is nothing less than grabbing onto the robe of the Maker of the universe. As you approach the Sabbath, a measure of awe is in order. The Sabbath is not part of a trendy self-help program. It is a part of heaven and a glimpse of God. Sabbath is not one day of vacation a week. It is part of the most solid and tangible time of life. The Sabbath balances the *active* parts of life with the *holy* parts. Jesus needed both to be fully human, and so do we.

Tools to Build a Sabbath Refuge

We've discussed the history of Sabbath. We've explored the rationale of 24/6 in a 24/7 world. We've talked about Sabbath in the Old and New Testaments. We've defined work and rest. We've seen how rest may actually help us live longer. And now we are getting to the part of *24/6* where we will build a refuge in the Sabbath.

But in order to construct something, one needs tools. When I was introduced to carpentry as a child, I was given a small tool set with a hammer, screwdriver, saw, and the like. They were substantial enough to cut soft wood, but not so deadly as to take something off without thinking.

Anything less than what I got would have been a toy, and anything more would have been dangerous.

When God began to teach the world about the Sabbath, he, too, started with simple tools. He began with a substance like shortbread. The details can be found in Exodus 16 and Numbers 11. Shopping malls and grocery stores have always been in short supply out on the Sinai Peninsula. It was even more so in Moses' day. So God made manna rain from the sky at night. Every morning the newly freed slaves went out to gather manna off the ground. If they picked up too little, it didn't matter; each family always had just enough. And God explicitly instructed them not to store manna overnight.

Despite this warning, some families still put manna in the refrigerator for the next day. In the morning, they knew better. Spoiled manna smelled worse than dead groundhog in a drainage ditch. It wasn't just that the manna went bad overnight, either. In addition to smelling like decaying groundhog, day-old manna crawled with maggots.

There was one exception to the overnight rule. God instructed the Hebrews to pick up a double portion of manna the day before Sabbath. In this way they would have enough for two days. They were told to bake manna for Sabbath the day beforehand because no housework was allowed on their day of rest.

On Sabbath morning, even when manna collected the day before was left out on the counter overnight, it still had that fresh-from-the-oven taste. The Sabbath was to be a day of rest: no shopping, cooking, or gathering manna.

Despite God's manna rules, some of the people still got up Sabbath morning and went looking for manna on the ground. But there was none to be found.

The echo of manna in the desert is heard when Christ is tempted in the wilderness. "Turn these stones into bread," the devil says to a starving Jesus. When Jesus replies, "No! . . . 'People do not live by bread alone, but by every word that comes from the mouth of God'" (Matthew 4:4), he is harking back to the time in the wilderness when his ancestors were learning what it was to be the people of God (see Deuteronomy 8:3). Although it is easier for us to understand the urgency of physical needs as opposed to spiritual ones, the Sabbath reminds us of both. It reassures us of God's love and care in all the areas of our lives.

Consider this passage from Deuteronomy:

> ¹Be careful to obey all the commands I am giving you today. Then you will live and multiply, and you will enter and occupy the land the LORD swore to give your ancestors. ²Remember how the LORD your God led you through the wilderness for these forty years, humbling you and testing you to prove your character, and to find out whether or not you would obey his commands. ³Yes, he humbled you by letting you go hungry and then feeding you with manna, a food previously unknown to you and your

ancestors. He did it to teach you that people do not live by bread alone; rather, we live by every word that comes from the mouth of the LORD. ⁴For all these forty years your clothes didn't wear out, and your feet didn't blister or swell. ⁵Think about it: Just as a parent disciplines a child, the LORD your God disciplines you for your own good.

⁶So obey the commands of the LORD your God by walking in his ways and fearing him. ⁷For the LORD your God is bringing you into a good land of flowing streams and pools of water, with fountains and springs that gush out in the valleys and hills. ⁸It is a land of wheat and barley; of grapevines, fig trees, and pomegranates; of olive oil and honey. ⁹It is a land where food is plentiful and nothing is lacking. It is a land where iron is as common as stone, and copper is abundant in the hills. ¹⁰When you have eaten your fill, be sure to praise the LORD your God for the good land he has given you.

¹¹But that is the time to be careful! Beware that in your plenty you do not forget the LORD your God and disobey his commands, regulations, and decrees that I am giving you today. ¹²For when you have become full and prosperous and have built fine homes to live in, ¹³and when your flocks and herds have become very large and your silver and gold have multiplied along with everything else, be careful! ¹⁴Do not become proud at that time and forget the

LORD your God, who rescued you from slavery in the land of Egypt. ¹⁵Do not forget that he led you through the great and terrifying wilderness with its poisonous snakes and scorpions, where it was so hot and dry. He gave you water from the rock! ¹⁶He fed you with manna in the wilderness, a food unknown to your ancestors. He did this to humble you and test you for your own good. ¹⁷He did all this so you would never say to yourself, "I have achieved this wealth with my own strength and energy." ¹⁸Remember the LORD your God. He is the one who gives you power to be successful, in order to fulfill the covenant he confirmed to your ancestors with an oath.

¹⁹But I assure you of this: If you ever forget the LORD your God and follow other gods, worshiping and bowing down to them, you will certainly be destroyed. ²⁰Just as the LORD has destroyed other nations in your path, you also will be destroyed if you refuse to obey the LORD your God. (Deuteronomy 8)

Remember that you were slaves in Egypt, and that you were delivered by the Lord. You were hungry, and the Lord cared enough to feed you himself. You were disciplined because you were loved. There is more to being human than just eating, drinking, and making merry. You are created in the Lord's image, and you need spiritual bread that can only come from the Lord. Don't spoil your appetite for the Lord's Supper by eating spiritual junk food.

Americans currently live more than twice as long as our country's founding mothers and fathers did. We have twenty to thirty times more income. We have so much food that we are in far more danger of eating ourselves to death than of going hungry. Many of our homes are enormous. We are as a whole better educated than people at any other time in history.

Yet glance at verses 12 through 14 in the Scripture above. The warning has relevance to us today. Prosperity can be as dangerous as poverty to our souls. In good times, we begin to think that all we have results from our own cleverness and ingenuity. No one ever found the Lord on the day they won the lottery. Faith is more likely to blossom on the day we lose our job.

We need the Sabbath for the perspective it gives us. You have more than you think if you think you have too little, and you have less than you think if you believe you have it all.

In my experience, Sabbath encourages thankfulness without the wake-up call of illness, loss, or ruin. It allows me to see miracles. It increases my sense of wonder. During the workweek, I sometimes struggle with my faith. Where is God? But on the Sabbath, I feel the Lord's presence. My cup runneth over; my batteries are charged. Sabbath reminds me that God is the source of my life. When we go 24/7, we get to thinking that our well-being results from our own efforts. God gets taken out of the equation. We lose track of who made the universe. We begin thinking that the world can't run without us.

Both poverty and wealth can threaten our faith and relationship with the Lord. Sabbath is the great equalizer. It is a balancing point. On the Sabbath the poor man is wealthy and the rich are to be humble. We need the Sabbath for the perspective it gives us. You have more than you think if you think you have too little, and you have less than you think if you believe you have it all. Sabbath gives that kind of balance.

Time for Friendship

I have traveled a great deal in the last several years. I've been able to meet people all over the country. Many are involved in the church. They range from folks in the pews to pastors and missionaries to seminary professors. They are a wonderful group. But no matter how much we have in common, I don't have the same relationship with them that is possible with people I see over and over again. Friendship takes time.

On Sabbath we come to rest, and we draw near to the Lord. We retreat. We spend time together. It is an appropriate time for prayer, church, and Bible reading. But something even more intimate happens on Stop Day. There is time for just being with the Lord.

When I am alone with someone new, like when I've

been picked up at the airport, I make polite conversation. That's what's required when you are just meeting someone. It's called small talk. When I'm with old friends, or with Nancy and the kids, we catch up and reconnect, but then we also talk about things of importance. If we have sufficient time, we get to comfortable silence—the "you say it best when you say nothing at all" time.

The same happens with God. When I don't have much time to spend with God, I get started with small talk. I let God know what I'm worried about and what I'm thankful for. I don't think there's anything wrong with that, nor do I see any advice counter to this in the Bible. But just as with family, it's the part beyond the small talk that restores my soul. It's not small talk but God-sized quiet time that defines my intimacy with the Lord. You need quality *and* quantity time to make intimacy happen. Fortunately God designed our schedules to accommodate both.

In the 24/7 world, we "pencil" friends in on the calendar. These loose commitments frequently fail to materialize. We have the best of intentions, but intentions don't build relationships. Filling in every Sunday on our calendar with "FOR THE LORD" in permanent ink changes our perspective. Honoring a Sabbath every week makes us more committed and serious about our relationship with the Lord. This is even more crucial today, when things travel as fast as the speed of light. God designed us to spend one day a week at the speed of stop.

Jesus is the most reproduced action figure of all time.

Chef, teacher, healer, tournament fishing champ—Jesus did more in three years than most people get done in a lifetime. But he knew how to stop. He stole away to spend time doing nothing but being with God. And he kept the Sabbath every week of his life.

We admire a work ethic. Our Savior had it. Our country is built on it. But it may be that, as for the Hebrews in the desert who hoarded and thought they could bend the rules, the manna has turned to maggots. Maybe living in a 24/7 world is too much. Maybe 24/6 is enough.

In the 24/7 world, we "pencil" friends in on the calendar. Filling in every Sunday on our calendar with "FOR THE LORD" in permanent ink makes us more committed and serious about our relationship with the Lord.

Todd Dowell worked after losing three fingers. But he is not alone. I've seen similar cases of patients walking out the door in the midst of heart attacks because they were worried about a business deal. I've seen wealthy parents leave sick children to fend for themselves while they go off to earn more. People try to take their money with them when they die, and zillionaires work up to the day of their funerals stuffing their piggy banks.

For the most part, people in our culture do not need more. We need to recognize how much we have. The Sabbath is a reality check. It says you have enough. Try to get more, and your manna will turn to maggots.

PART 4

Your 24/6 Life

Don't Forget the Sabbath

Don't forget the Sabbath,
The Lord our God hath blest,
Of all the week the brightest,
Of all the week the best;
It brings repose from labor,
It tells of joy divine,
Its beams of light descending,
With heav'nly beauty shine.

Welcome, welcome, ever welcome,
Blessed Sabbath day.
Welcome, welcome, ever welcome,
Blessed Sabbath day.

Keep the Sabbath holy,
And worship him today,
Who said to his disciples,
"I am the Living Way";
And if we meekly follow
Our Savior here below,
He'll give us of the Fountain
Whose streams eternal flow.

Day of sacred pleasure!
Its golden hours we'll spend
In thankful hymns to Jesus,
The children's dearest Friend;
O gentle, loving, Savior,
How good and kind thou art,
How precious is thy promise
To dwell in ev'ry heart!

Fanny Crosby

CHAPTER 10

The Sermon on the Amount

This is what the LORD says: "Be just and fair to all. Do what
is right and good, for I am coming soon to rescue you and
to display my righteousness among you. Blessed are all those
who are careful to do this. Blessed are those who honor my
Sabbath days of rest and keep themselves from doing wrong."

Isaiah 56:1-2

SATURDAY EVENING has finally arrived. We finish our
work, clean the house, and walk to the grocery store. I am
tired. It has been a week of travel and intense meetings, but
that is no excuse for what happens next.

Nancy shops while I push the cart through the narrow
aisles. When she finishes, she leaves me and the cart in a
checkout line to track down one more item. The tabloids
and magazines feature an immodest display for inquiring
minds; the racks beside them offer dozens of candy bars.
I wonder what to do if my turn comes and Nancy is
not back.

Tom, our cashier, begins to ring up the woman directly

in front of me. She's dressed modestly, with her hair covered in Muslim fashion. I hear Tom ask if she's walking all the way home to Tates Creek Road and Alumni Drive. *That's quite a hike. Should I offer her a ride?* I start to interrupt and then remember that we arrived on foot. Nancy comes and adds an item to the basket. She asks, "Do you want me to pick out a movie for tonight?" I nod, and off Nancy goes to get one.

Something is holding up the line. The computer won't clear the woman's check. Our cashier recruits another employee. They punch in codes, but the machine still refuses her check. The woman reassures them that the check is good. The manager is on his way. He puts the check into and out of the machine. *Do I have that much cash with me?* I hesitate. *Should I tell her that we live only a few blocks away and will come back and give her a lift home?* I'm not sure. Suddenly, the woman pulls the groceries out of her backpack, flowers and all, and is out the door, empty handed.

I burn with shame as I realize that I didn't act first and think later. My wish-I-hads and should-haves are many: *I wish I had put her groceries on my charge card; she could have sent us the money later. I should have simply given her the groceries.*

That night I do not relish the coming of Sabbath as I usually do. I cannot let it go. In the morning, I do not wake up to the peace that usually greets me. I call my friend John and tell him the story. "Matthew, what were you thinking?" he wants to know. I can hear the disappointment in his voice. He expects more of me.

And so does God, *especially* on Sabbath eve. Sabbath and giving are two sides of the same coin. They intersect at Abraham's camp, at Solomon's Temple, and at the Cross. Christianity links them when the offering plate is placed on the table with the elements of the Lord's Supper. This is no accident.

Sabbath was given to the Hebrews in the desert, and they gave Sabbath to the world. By the time of Christ, the Jewish day of rest had spread far and wide. The Greek writer Philo (20 BC–AD 50) noted, "Who has not shown his high respect for that sacred seventh day, by giving rest and relaxation from labor to himself and his neighbors, freemen and slaves alike, and beyond these to his beasts?" Roman statesman and philosopher Seneca (4 BC–AD 65) reported that the customs of the Jews "have gained such influence that they are now received throughout all the world. The vanquished have given laws to their victors." In Rome, Josephus (AD 37–100) wrote that there was "not any city of Greeks, nor any of the barbarians, nor any nation whatsoever" where the Sabbath was not observed.

As we know from Paul's writings, early Christians did not have it easy. Monotheistic Jews stoned them, and polytheistic pagans accused them of not getting stoned. They were used as fuel in the lamps at Nero's parties. Others were served up as lion food in the Coliseum. Romans discriminated against Christians when they hired, and they wouldn't approve their mortgages. Yet Christianity grew. Even their detractors begrudgingly admitted that the Christians had one great attribute: they were generous. It is not surprising, then, that much discussion in Acts and the Epistles centers on taking up collections.

Giving money to others makes no worldly sense. It is therefore on equal footing with the Sabbath. When we grant others Sabbath rest, we act as God's anointed agents. The longest of the Ten Commandments tells us to keep the Sabbath, but the majority of its verbiage is about giving the Sabbath away.

Giving money to others makes no worldly sense. It is therefore on equal footing with the Sabbath.

For a believer, there is no separating the Sabbath and giving. They are conjoined twins that share the same heart. The "work" accomplished on our day of rest is not just the renewal of our souls, but the recharging of our impulse to give. When we grant others a day of rest, not only do we act in obedience, we act in generosity. It is good to take a Sabbath; it is godly to give one.

Unfortunately, Christians have a mixed record as far as giving their Sabbath away is concerned. Ask people who work in a restaurant when their least favorite time is to wait tables. "After church on Sundays" is what you'll hear. The workers in the restaurant don't complain that we're demanding or rude. What they find fault with is our lack of generosity. There is no time when the teachings of the church are fresher in our minds, yet what have we learned if we stiff the waitress an hour after we leave the pew? How much worse will our behavior be twenty-four hours later?

If you get nothing else from this book, please, double down when it comes time to tip after church! Better still, go with a 50-percent or 100-percent tip. If that kind of generosity got to be the rule, how long do you think it would take until everyone in the food industry began wondering what's going on at church?

My observation is that generally those who keep a Sabbath also tithe. Both practices stem from a worldview of abundance. Perhaps after keeping one counterintuitive practice, the Sabbath keeper or tithe giver better understands the benefits of the other.

The anger I felt toward myself when I failed to pay for the woman's groceries faded after a few days. But my regret at missing a chance to be blessed has not. I put nothing in the soil, and so nothing grew. Paul explained this to the church at Corinth:

> Remember this—a farmer who plants only a few seeds will get a small crop. But the one who plants generously will get a generous crop. You must each decide in your heart how much to give. And don't give reluctantly or in response to pressure. "For God loves a person who gives cheerfully." And God will generously provide all you need. Then you will

always have everything you need and plenty left over
to share with others. (2 Corinthians 9:6-8)

It is better to give than to receive, but I did neither in
that checkout line. We are blessed to be a blessing. The
Sabbath is meant to be given away.

Advice for Those Who Get Paid to Pray

Thirty-one years ago, Pastor Gerald stepped into the pulpit
of his large Atlanta church and made an announcement.
"Today is Sunday," he said. "This is the day that the Lord
hath made. We come together today to worship the Lord.
But I have an announcement to make about Mondays. From
now on, you may not get married on Mondays. You may not
get sick on Mondays. You may die then, but I won't bury
you. My wife and I are going to Sabbath on Mondays."

Gerald says that this announcement changed the course
of his life. It also changed his ministry. His proclamation
said that he was no longer in charge: God was taking over
senior management of the church.

A similar story is told by Eugene Peterson, best known
for his Bible paraphrase, *The Message*. He asked his congregation to help him keep a Sabbath. He didn't guilt them.
He just said he needed it, and the people needed him.
In his book to pastors, *Working the Angles*, Peterson talks
about the difference between *playing* pastor and *being* pastor. He notes that the congregation will applaud either.

Listeners may not be able to tell the difference between a pastor who is preaching and one who is merely pretending to preach, but the pastor can. Sabbath keeping allows church leaders to recall why they are called.

I found a similar phenomenon in medicine. Despite the high pay, good social standing, and trust from patients, many doctors go through the day like zombies—too worn out to recognize the miracles taking place around them. Patients used to die from appendicitis and complications in childbirth. Giving an antibiotic or immunization is nothing short of magic. But if doctors don't appreciate that they are dispensing miracles, how will their patients?

The same is true for pastors. The whole church is in trouble when those in leadership forget that they are in the miracle business. Sabbath is a weekly reminder of all that is good in God's world. Make sure your church is generous with its workers. Don't support a spiritual sweatshop.

Friday Is Just a Hop, Skip, and a Jump Away from Sunday

We have looked at how the Sabbath and giving are inextricably linked. Let's go one step further. Giving and Sabbath are primary ingredients of hospitality. Let me explain.

Among my wife's many fine qualities is an ability to extend hospitality to others. Notice that I didn't say "to entertain others." Entertaining is about the host; hospitality is about the guest. These are two different things.

Hospitality allows us to enjoy the company of those with whom we may have little in common. Much in our culture panders to the lowest level of human interaction: finding our differences. What party do you support? What color jersey does your team wear? Hospitality asks us to put aside differences. Hospitality demands that we find common ground.

We often have guests at our table. These guests come from different countries, different political traditions, and different socioeconomic groups. Some have different faiths, and some have no faith. Some have good table manners— and some not so much. Some are picky eaters, and some had good moms who taught them to eat everything on their plates.

Many of these guests share our family's Friday night dinners. I used to make no connection between our Friday evenings and the Sabbath. After all, they are separated by a day. Then two things happened. First, our children grew up and moved out. Second, our lives got busier.

As a result, we were no longer eating meals together as a family. Clark had to balance medical school, church on Saturday nights, and his wife's weekend teaching. Emma graduated, got an apartment with her college roommate, and began developing her own circles and routines. Nancy and I started a ministry that grew from a mom-and-pop operation to a national organization. Dinner with family got to be hit or miss. We had people over to eat and I saw the children frequently, but I longed for regular contact.

We needed a time everyone could count on being together. For many families, that day is Sunday. But the problem with our family getting together on Sundays is that I am often off preaching on that day. So we started having dinner at our house every Friday night.

Friday night family dinners are not a new invention, but they are rare in today's overcommitted culture. In a perfect world, we would invent new things and then have the wisdom to know if they were worth keeping. We would have the very best of a thousand generations. Nothing great would be lost, and nothing bad would be preserved. In an ideal world, we would have both Hebrew Sabbath evenings and Christian Sunday mornings.

In getting together every Friday, our family stumbled onto something wonderful about the rhythm of Jesus' life. Hebrew Sabbath begins at sundown at the end of the workweek. It starts with a meal. By definition this is an intimate time.

In a world of specialization and compartmentalization, the Sabbath is a freeing oasis with a gushing spring. It allows God to flow into all of my week.

Friday evenings in our home have a ritual holiness about them. We didn't plan it that way, but that's the way it is. We talk and laugh. We save room for dessert. I get to know my children as adults, and I see them through the eyes of others. Our guests include people we have met in our travels, friends of our children, and students studying at the university in need of a home-cooked meal and a seat at the table with an intact family. Over the years, our children have learned to find common ground with people from widely diverse backgrounds.

In a way, our Sabbath begins on Friday evenings. We work Saturdays and rest on Sundays. Keeping a Sabbath every week is one of the reasons Nancy and I can be as productive as we are. Sabbath has spilled into our Fridays, and the energy of Sabbath flows into our Mondays and beyond.

Sabbath leads to giving, and giving leads to hospitality. The Sabbath makes way for joy and contemplation, and that allows us to hear God. After keeping Sabbath for a decade, we no longer see our weekly rest as a discrete day but as a sabbatical way of life.

In a world of specialization and compartmentalization, the Sabbath is a freeing oasis with a gushing spring. It allows God to flow into all of my week.

Hospitality on a Biblical Scale: A Modern Parable

All of history veered when Abraham woke from his nap at the Mamre Fairgrounds. God knows why he did. Perhaps it was a rustling of fabric. Maybe it was the quiet or stillness. The dog wagged its tail instead of barking as it normally would.

How long had Abraham been dozing there by the camper? It was hot, the sun high in the blue sky. He looked up and saw three men. They didn't appear threatening, but they didn't seem afraid, either. Abraham stood and walked out from under the huge oaks. He went to the strangers and bowed low. "Come and sit"—he motioned toward the lawn chairs—"be my guests." They nodded and moved into the shade. "Will you stay for dinner?"

Yes, the three said, that would suit them. Abraham called to the boy on the swing. "Go and get Eliezer."

Abraham motioned to a teenager to take off his earphones. "Tell the servants to get iced tea for the guests. Then get some water to wash these men's feet."

"But Father, the well is low. I thought you said not to waste water."

"Don't say anything in front of the guests," Abraham whispered to Ishmael. The old man stuck his head in the screen door. "Sarah, make some bread. Don't use the flour from that soft grindstone; use the batch Lot sent for your ninetieth. And take the Cabot cheese out of the icebox so that it can warm up."

"Are you sure you want a fire? I thought you said the heat has been getting to you," Sarah countered.

"Don't worry about the heat. We've got guests." Abraham turned and met his servant Eliezer, who was hurrying down the slope.

"Eliezer, kill the large calf, and have someone light the fire so that it can burn down and we won't char the bread and meat," Abraham said as he headed back to the three guests.

"I thought you wanted Ishmael to enter that calf in the

fair next month," Eliezer questioned as he pointed to the largest calf of the herd.

"No, we've got guests. Enter that one," said Abraham, pointing to the second largest calf in the pen.

The Trinity sipped tea and ate appetizers off Egyptian trays. Then Abraham brought out the main course. Since those first ones, billions and billions have been served, but they are all poor imitations compared to the cheeseburgers made of fresh veal and served on warm bread (Genesis 18).

Abraham entertaining the angels may not have occurred on the Sabbath—the Fourth Commandment had not been given yet, so we'll never know—but it certainly models the spirit of Sabbath giving. God is our host here on earth, and Sabbath is his gift to us. He gives us both the place and the time to celebrate with him. Fortunately for us, Sabbath occurs week after week, so we are given thousands of opportunities to get it right.

A few weeks after I blew my opportunity to help in the checkout line, God offered me another chance. Nancy and I were out on our Sabbath walk when a man approached us. His shoes were in tatters.

God didn't have to dummy slap me twice. This time, I knew what to do.

"God bless you," the man said as we parted.

"He just has," I answered.

CHAPTER 11

Let the Celebration Begin

Come unto me, all ye that labour and are heavy laden, and I
will give you rest. Take my yoke upon you, and learn of me;
for I am meek and lowly in heart: and ye shall find rest unto
your souls. For my yoke is easy, and my burden is light.

Matthew 11:28-30, KJV

MAGGIE PLUMMER sat on the exam table looking as for-
lorn as anyone in North America. Great skeins of reddish
hair framed her disheartened five-year-old face. Her shoulders were slumped and her cheeks tearstained. You could
park a Buick on her pouting lower lip. Her chart listed ear
pain as the chief complaint. Maggie's father sat holding her
twin in his lap. They looked identical: hair, faces, misery,
and all.

"Do they both have an earache?" I queried.

"Not yet, but they will," their father explained. "They're
mirror twins, and they do everything together, even getting
sick. When Maggie gets an ear infection on the right, Lila

will get one on the left. If this is like all the other ear infections they've had, in twenty-four hours they'll both have a fever and won't be able to keep anything down."

He paused. "We told them that we'll have to cancel their birthday party tomorrow." Both Maggie and Lila's lower lips began to wibble in sync.

"Let's get a look," I said, as I took the otoscope off the wall. "You mind if I check your ears too?" I asked Lila, the one who wasn't hurting. She held her locks at bay, tilted her head, and presented a charming little ear. I looked at one tympanic membrane and then her other. "Looks perfect, and I can really see her eardrums well."

I popped on a new ear speculum, turned to Maggie, and looked in the left ear. "This one's great." Then I gently took hold of her right ear. The ear canal was swollen, and the view of the eardrum was blocked.

"She's got a little rock in the canal," I said. "When did this start bothering her?"

"It was after they were swimming in the pond two days ago," her father answered. "At first we thought she'd just gotten some water stuck in it, but it kept getting worse. We figured it was another ear infection."

I got out the suctioning equipment that is made for just this sort of thing. In a jiff we'd delivered the stone that had stirred off the bottom of the pond, lodged in her ear, and threatened to ruin her party. For the first time in two days, Maggie could hear out of the ear and had no pain.

I've seen the reaction of children and parents as I've

pulled M&Ms, LEGOs, and pistachios from noses. I've flushed out everything from cockroaches to spiders from ear canals. I well remember the look on one mother's face when I found a huge piece of foam compressed in her tike's nostril. But I had never seen the look that Maggie gave Lila when they realized the consequence of what had just happened.

"Any reason they can't have their party tomorrow?" Dad asked for them.

"No reason," I said, "as long as I get a birthday hug."

You may own the Chrysler Building, but brother, you haven't lived until you've been hugged—in stereo—by five-year-old girls who've just had their birthday party restored.

Sabbath is like a redeemed holiday (holy day) fifty-two times a year. It is a time to rejoice and celebrate. The parallel Bible scene that comes to mind is when Christ looks at the chart and sees "can't hear or speak" listed as the chief complaint:

> Jesus led him away from the crowd so they could be alone. He put his fingers into the man's ears. Then, spitting on his own fingers, he touched the man's tongue. Looking up to heaven, he sighed and said, "*Ephphatha*," which means, "Be opened!" Instantly the man could hear perfectly, and his tongue was freed so he could speak plainly! (Mark 7:33-35)

At first glance, we might think that Christ is merely opening the ears or perhaps the mouth of the speechless man. But he is just as surely performing an even greater miracle. He is throwing wide the gates of heaven. He is welcoming this man into the Kingdom. Amazing grace— how sweet the sound!

In a similar way, Christ draws us aside on the Sabbath day. He touches our ears and our tongues and helps us see the world differently. "*Ephphatha!*" echoes down a two-thousand-year-old information superhighway. "Be opened!" rings out, and the most magnificent of gifts is unwrapped. The gates to the Kingdom fall open, and it is left to us to step inside.

"But as for Me and My Family, We Will Serve the LORD"

Some of the questions that come up most about 24/6 involve parenting. Raising kids is no picnic. Parenting is *work*. How do parents both honor the Sabbath and perform the duties associated with their role as parents? As anyone with children knows, little kids can be exhausting. The first few years of parenthood is a season of life like no other. The work of parenting is 24/7. It doesn't escape even a casual reader of Genesis that Adam and Eve were childless before the Fall. So isn't it fitting that the birth of children takes place in a section of the hospital called "Labor and Delivery"?

Work and deliverance: a succinct summary of parenting. Tikes must be fed, changed, and nurtured around the clock. That's the "labor." But there is also deliverance. Parenting frees us—or at least offers us the chance to be free—from our self-centeredness.

I used to work with an older nurse who was an absolute expert on parenting. She could spot problems and offer parenting solutions with astounding clarity and conviction. There was only one problem: she'd never had children.

My advice about how to honor the Sabbath while parenting young children is to seek wisdom from those who have a proven track record. To this end, I talked with our friend Bethany Barker, wife of Keith and mother of Ela, Jake, and Oren (ages seven, five, and two) about their Sabbath traditions. Bethany sets out special cinnamon "Sabbath bread" on Saturday night. On Sunday morning, the kids get up and Ela reads the instructions that Bethany has left for them. After feeding themselves, they play with a special box of toys while Bethany and Keith enjoy some extra rest.

The Barkers have made a number of career and lifestyle choices that enhance their Sabbath. They live near extended family, and almost every Sunday a dozen of them get together for lunch. The kids play with cousins while the adults catch up. The Barkers also intentionally sought out a small, family-oriented church close to home that meets late Sunday afternoons. After playing with cousins and church buddies, the kids are often in bed early on Sunday evenings. Bethany relates that the meal and conversation that she and Keith share on Sunday night is the highlight of their week.

While I don't think there is a magic formula for keeping the Sabbath with young children, I do believe that small rituals—like Sunday cinnamon bread or a box of quiet toys that can be used only on Sundays—set the tone for later years. And I believe that something wonderful happens when mothers of young children get together and share what works for them. So much of modern life is about isolation and competition. Sabbathing lends itself to community and cooperation.

As children age, Sabbath traditions change and grow accordingly. When our children lived at home, they attended a rigorous high school. In order to both take off one day a week *and* keep up with school, they were often up before dawn on weekdays. It sounds tough. It *was* tough. But unlike their classmates, our children had at least one guilt-free day off every week.

On a number of occasions my daughter and I have spoken together at churches. Emma is asked one question repeatedly that she doesn't know how to answer. It goes something like this: "The problem with my kids is that they will only do what their friends do. How do I get my children to be more like you?"

Emma loves her family. She loves God. She wrote a book when she was fifteen and graduated from college at nineteen. At twenty-one, she's involved in her church, wholesome, and respectful of her elders. She can't help but brag about her big brother, the doctor. It's no wonder that folks want their daughters to be more like her. But when she gets asked this question, she doesn't know what to say. She can't be honest *and* polite to the adult who has asked the question. She's in a bind. Moreover, she knows that being asked this by a parent points to the underlying problem: you don't ask children how to raise children; you ask their parents.

Young people are leaving the church in droves—something like 70 percent during the college years. Various explanations are given. Some say it is because of music or movies. Others cite exposure to modern technology and short attention spans. Churches have adapted by installing laser-light disco balls and delivering twelve-minute messages. But the exodus continues. One reason is that most children do exactly what they are taught—and they see their parents worshiping many lesser gods.

My children had to work hard to keep a Sabbath in high school and college. It meant they couldn't participate in every school activity. If the choice came between a team, game, or test and honoring the Sabbath, we honored the Sabbath.

Though at first it may sound counterintuitive, raising children to keep the Sabbath means you work *less* as a parent in the long run. It's the real-world application of the fun-size candy bar now or the giant-size one later. Jesus said he would give rest to those who labored and were heavy laden. No group in our society labors harder than parents who raise children to serve multiple gods.

Children learn more from what their parents do than from what we say. We may hang a Joshua 24:15 plaque on the wall, but if our kids see us go to church for an hour and then spend the entire week worshiping other gods,

We may hang a Joshua 24:15 plaque on the wall, but if our kids see us go to church for an hour and then spend the entire week worshiping other gods, what message will they internalize?

what message will they internalize? How well are we and our houses serving the Lord when we break the Fourth Commandment week in, week out?

Suppose your child tells you on Sunday afternoon that he needs red poster board for a project due on Monday. Because you want to model a loving and forgiving God, on the first or second occasion, you might explain the importance of preparing for the Sabbath and then make a trip to the store. But over the long haul, it's easier to teach lessons while they are inexpensive. A missed school project is an inexpensive way to learn the lessons of Sabbath: school, sports, teachers, children, mothers-in-law, and parents are not the head of the house. God is.

Ultimately, all other gods give less and exact more. The Third Commandment says that God will not tolerate the worship of idols. Bad parenting will haunt four generations of children, but letting God head the house will result in a thousand generations of blessings.

Parenting is perhaps the hardest—and most important—work of all. Let the Lord of the Sabbath and his day do some of the heavy lifting for you.

Going to Church

Another way to step into the Sabbath is to step into another home: the house of God. One of the great gifts I've been granted is the privilege of visiting hundreds of churches. These range in size from micro to macro. They encompass a wide theological spectrum; Baptists, Methodists, Salvationists, Presbyterians, and many others have lent me their pulpits.

The apostle Paul referred to the church as a "body" in his first letter to the Corinthians. The parts of our bodies that we curl, make up, and blow-dry are really not as important to us as the parts we cover with underwear, he admonishes in the twelfth chapter. The foot can't say, "I'm not a part of the body" because it is not a hand. Every part is important and benefits the body as a whole.

In the first century AD, no one knew about the adrenal or pineal glands. They didn't understand the workings of the endocrine or the exocrine systems. But God knew. The metaphors of the Bible are just as true today as they were in Paul's time.

We have a living Bible—a book written for all ages. Our understanding of the truth may advance, but all truth is God's truth. No part of a body can live without the others. A cell on the ground or one frozen in a test tube may *exist*, but it can never *grow* without being a part of a greater whole.

So while this book is not about church, my advice is to

belong to one. You can exist as a Christian without one, but you won't reach your full potential. Few of us grow alone as well as we can within a body of believers. For most people, participating in a church is an important way of keeping the Sabbath holy.

The Sermon at the Food Court

Stepping into the Sabbath usually involves stepping out of other things. In general, I avoid any commercial activity on my Sabbath. Five minutes at the mall can destroy five hours of sublime communion with God. Commerce and stopping don't mix, which is why the strongest reaction from Christ involved driving vendors from the Temple.

Traveling around the country, I've met wonderful people, encountered reverent prayer, and listened to music so beautiful it makes the angels weep. I've been confronted with deep questions, such as, "How did theologians of old come up with the concept of purgatory without being stuck overnight at O'Hare Airport?" I've been blessed to be part of many great worship services and small prayer groups. But they all looked like spiritual slackers compared to the Pentecostal worship I saw in the sky.

The prayers started one evening when the pilot of our small plane flew into the wake of a large jet. When our plane listed on its side and began falling out of the sky, the Lord's name was on every tongue—though on some more reverently than others.

That was the most heartfelt prayer service I have ever witnessed, but the most significant *sermon* occurred back on the ground, right in the middle of an airport food court. I was flying home on a Sunday after preaching (back when I often had to shift my Sabbaths because of weekend travel). My last leg had a layover at the Cincinnati airport. Douglas Adams once said that no language on earth has ever produced the saying "as pretty as an airport." Adams's observation is even truer for an airport food court filled to the brim with hungry weekend travelers. It was a sight to make one's eyes sore and to test one's faith: *Jesus died for* this?

In the midst of this feeding frenzy, I heard a sermon. The theme was the Fourth Commandment. While every food vendor was cashing in, one restaurant was closed. They eschewed profits on earth in favor of those in heaven.

Many businesses close one day a week. In shutting their doors, they declare their faith. They say that something is more important than profit. The customer is not always right. One day a week, God is.

One of the most impressive Sabbath-keeping businesses is B&H Photo in New York City. In addition to closing their seventy-thousand-square-foot retail business on the Sabbath, B&H shuts down their extensive Internet sales for twenty-four hours each week. Their example reminds us that Sabbath is not just a rest from work; it is a break from commerce.

Chick-fil-A, Hobby Lobby, B&H Photo, and many

other businesses close one day a week. In shutting their doors, they declare their faith. They say that something is more important than profit. The customer is not always right. One day a week, God is.

Sometimes inaction speaks louder than words. If you believe in 24/6, find businesses that close one day a week and patronize them on the other six.

Be Still and Know That I Am God

Sabbath is about awe and wonder—a reflection of God. If you aren't seeing miracles on a daily basis, it might be helpful to take notes.

I keep a running list of things I've seen throughout the week that remind me of God. On Sabbath, I read the list. The more I add to the notes, the more I realize God is dishing out miracles all the time. When a visual record will help, I grab a photo with my phone. My notes on God consist of pictures, questions, observations, and musings. Here are a few miracles I've recorded in my notebook:

- Two boys in a swing wound up by their older sister. What joy they get spinning round and coming down!
- The tenacity of the squirrel that outsmarts my bird feeder placement. IQs of Einstein in the air—not so much in the road.
- The moon always keeps its face to us. What would the world be like if it rotated twice a night?

- The sandhill crane that can out-yoga a yogi. But Nancy tries to match it, standing on one foot as long as the crane.
- A group of young people in the airport playing cards; one jumps for joy and shouts, "Uno!" Make a joyful sound to the Lord.
- Six-year-old Isaac asks me if the pharaoh was still alive when I was little. There is a look of disappointment in his eyes when I say, "No, I never met the pharaoh." I guess I am now officially OLD.

When I was in medical school, I saw patient after interesting patient. It was their stories more than their diagnoses that I found so compelling. I'd get together with my friend Alan and compare notes. We both had unbelievable luck. Our classmates were envious. They got the boring patients. But Alan's and my good fortune held. This happened rotation after rotation.

I didn't believe in God then, and I wasn't superstitious. Still, even I could tell there was something going on. It wasn't statistically possible to get all the great patients. I began to keep a record of interesting cases in my daily planner. It took several years for me to puzzle out why Alan and I were so fortunate: most patients are great; you just have to see them that way. If Buck Rogers showed up in many doctors' waiting rooms, they wouldn't ask how space was, or if they could play with his ray gun. The trick is to look for the stories. Whether by accident, providence, or grace, my list of interesting cases was the first batch of miracles I wrote down.

Nancy recently met a young woman who used her camera to record one beautiful thing she saw every day. She started to share them on Facebook. Soon it got to be work: she felt pressure to find a miracle every day and record it. Like her quest, even the best-intentioned tools—including a list of everyday miracles—can become a drudge. So how do we maintain our sense of wonder and awe?

God rarely shows up at the foot of our beds and wakes us from sleep. We must listen for God in the narrative of life. Stopping one day a week allows my hearing to improve. I pick up the subtle chorus of heaven here on earth. God speaks through his Scriptures and the lives contained in them, but he also speaks through our lives, wives, children, parents, friends, nature, music, food, trials, and triumphs.

God rarely shows up at the foot of our beds and wakes us from sleep. We must listen for God in the narrative of life. Stopping one day a week allows my hearing to improve.

As you map out your 24/6 practices, keep the end goal in mind—a holy day of rest. Is watching this show, reading a particular book, or going to a certain place holy? If not, is there something else—something more honest, pure, lovely, and of good report—that you could be doing instead?

I've met many people who use the meditative practice

of subtracting one word at a time from Psalm 46:10 to help them come to rest:

> Be still, and know that I am God.
> Be still, and know that I am.
> Be still, and know that I.
> Be still, and know that.
> Be still, and know.
> Be still, and.
> Be still.
> Be.

When we are young, like the twins Maggie and Lila, we instinctively know how to just *be*. As we grow older, we lose this ability. Sabbath is a time to transition from human *doings* to human *beings*. It is a day to celebrate a God who makes time for us to be with him.

CHAPTER 12

Shabbat Shalom

May the LORD bless you and protect you. May the
LORD smile on you and be gracious to you. May the
LORD show you his favor and give you his peace.

Numbers 6:24-26

THE BEGINNING of medical school is a big deal. Even if
you have a PhD—and about 10 percent of my class did—
you are going to work harder than you ever have before.

On the first day of school, we sat in a lecture hall and
listened to the dean explain who we were and where we'd
come from. We had snake handlers, lawyers, dentists, and
musicians among our ranks. We ranged in age from nineteen to forty. We even had an exotic dancer in our midst.

"Take a look up and down the rows," the dean said.
"One in ten of your classmates will not be with you when
you graduate in four years. It's not that they lack the
brains. We wouldn't have let them in if that were the case.

No—they lack the drive, the work ethic, or the character. It's up to you to decide whether you are going to be here come graduation day." We scanned up and down the rows, trying to tell if there was some giveaway. Was it a look in the eye? Was it a hairstyle or outfit that gave a hint? All of us were anxious to know: Who was the exotic dancer?

Sure enough, every semester—right up until the last—a couple of students were asked to leave. The take-home message wasn't about character; it was about working harder than the competition. This type of pyramid structure no longer exists in medical schools, but nothing has really changed.

My son's first week at medical school had a similar message to mine, even though it was more subtle. For his class, it snuck through in a session about finding balance. Three faculty members sat onstage and made a case for having a life outside of medical school. They told the class they would be better doctors and human beings if they got away from their studies on a regular basis.

As an example of what not to do, they cited the case of a medical student who never left the hospital in the last two clinical years. He worked like a demon, eating his meals from hospital vending machines. By the end of medical school, he'd gained a hundred pounds!

There was quiet as the case study sank in. Then one of Clark's classmates raised his hand and asked, "What became of this student?" The three faculty members glanced at each other, hesitating. Then the dean cleared his throat: "He graduated first in his class."

Such workaholism is common among physicians. I once attended a conference where a presenter tried to teach us doctors how to relax. We all closed our eyes and breathed in a special way. When the exercise was over, the leader pointed out that during our time relaxing, about half of us had peeked to see if anyone was more relaxed than we were. And so it goes. Doctors frequently complain about the hours they work and the number of patients they see. They wax Homeric in tales of battles with disease. Yet when they are offered positions with fewer hours, they shy away.

There is something comforting about being over-worked. If work is the meaning of our lives, then more work equals more meaning. Our work ethic even extends to our time away from work. We like to say that we work hard and we play hard. But 24/6 is not about working hard and playing hard. It is about working hard and stopping. In that rhythm, the work takes on more meaning, and the stopping takes on holiness.

> 24/6 is not about working hard and playing hard. It is about working hard and stopping.

We cannot work our way to heaven, but many of us try. The need to impress God is part of our fall from Eden. You will miss the take-home point of 24/6 if you work at impressing God on your Sabbath. The trick is to allow God to have the room, space, and quiet needed to make an impression on you.

Sleeth Sabbaths

When I am not traveling or preaching, we stop on Sundays. If and when we have to choose a different day, we find that Fridays or Saturdays work better than Mondays. Folks seem to let it pass when you don't return calls or e-mails on Fridays, but this is less true for Mondays.

We finish our work on Sabbath eve. We visit the grocery store two blocks away. We do a liturgical cleaning of the house. It is important that our home is organized and well stocked for Sunday; we don't want to be sidelined by unfinished chores. If we plan to drive somewhere for a hike, I fill up the tank. Nancy has a ritual of clearing off her desk and closing her computer. I take off the wristwatch she gave me thirty years ago.

On Sabbath eves we go to bed early or late, depending on our level of exhaustion. It is a wonderful thing to luxuriate in the knowledge that the Sabbath stretches out in front of us. I like to think of it as a magical time room. When we close the door and throw the latch, the world outside comes to a halt. We can read entire novels, and not a moment passes. We are wealthy with time. Only fools or misers would derive pleasure from counting money once they were rich. It is the same for those who finally find themselves in possession of the chronologic fortune that the Sabbath represents. If we want to stay up until the wee hours of the morning listening to music, we can afford the time.

The same goes for getting up. If we wake before the sun rises, why not get up and go for a walk? We can always take a nap later. On the other hand, if we still feel tired, we can roll over and go back to sleep.

One Sunday morning I awoke and lay in bed puzzling my way through a theme that spanned broad swaths of the Bible. It was wonderful. I thought and thought. I wrestled with the Scriptures. I tried to project myself back in time to better understand. I thought about how I would convey the concept in a sermon. I projected forward by several hundred years to get a hint of what God might be saying about the future. Then it struck me that I had not said my morning prayer. I stopped and began to pray.

Only fools or misers would derive pleasure from counting money once they were rich. It is the same for those who finally find themselves in possession of the chronologic fortune that the Sabbath represents.

Seldom do I get an overpowering and direct sense of the presence of the Lord, but I did then. It was as if God had said, "Matthew, why did you interrupt our conversation?" Conversation can be prayer. When we are having a great conversation—whether it is with the Lord or with a friend—we need not interrupt to gain control, get credit, or win approval.

What do we eat on Sunday morning? Cheerios with frozen peaches and one scoop of ice cream works for me. Nancy eats chocolate as her Sunday treat. I imbibe one soda. We don't labor over elaborate meals.

Many parents have a set of toys, books, or movies that children are allowed to enjoy only on the Sabbath. I have a book that I read only on that day. Right now, my Sunday book is the musings of Samuel Johnson. For several years, Nancy has read through the Bible each year, doing a majority of her reading on Sabbaths. Because I read and work from the Bible the other six days, I do not pick up the Good Book on my Sabbaths—but this is not a hard-and-fast rule. I particularly enjoy the peace and quiet that settles over our city on Sunday mornings, so we are often out for a long walk early in the day.

As a doctor, I recommend the habit of walking. Nancy and I walk most days, but the Sabbath strolls are special. A hike is good, too, but walks are essential. The difference between a hike and a walk is where you put your feet. On a hike you pay attention to the trail; on a walk you wind along wherever your feet happen to take you. I mostly walk on Nancy's right because she is deaf in her left ear. If we wish to walk in silence, I walk on her left. We have been walking, talking, arguing, and loving for over three decades. We are growing old together. We have been through much: college, medical school, death, and birth. It has not been easy. When we became followers of Christ about a decade ago, our walks adjusted to accommodate another: God is walking with us.

When I began to take one day off every week, I was not a follower of Christ. Yet I found a spiritual benefit. I wanted to share the wonderful aspects of the day with the people I worked with in the hospital. I found that we were great about listening to one another's tales of woe, over-work, purchases, action-packed vacations, and failing mar-riages, but we didn't have the language to talk about quiet, relaxation, love, and rest. The church often shies away from these topics as well.

Ironically, the most known and recited Psalm (Psalm 23) is about being led to still waters, green pastures, and sway-ing hammocks. Jesus sends an engraved invitation to those who feel overworked, oppressed, and heavy laden and says that those who make peace are the children of God.

When I married into a Jewish family decades ago, I was introduced to new customs, great food, and an ancient greeting: *Shabbat shalom*. *Shabbat shalom* is a way of wish-ing a fellow keeper of the Sabbath the peace (*shalom*) of Sabbath. But the greeting evokes more than peace: it also connotes wholeness, accord, and gentleness.

Shabbat shalom draws us toward the day when we will be separated neither from one another nor from God. It reminds us of a holistic and a holy peace. No one can truly be full while another hungers. Our wealth is not measured by what we own but by what the least among us has. *Shabbat shalom* is what we seek for ourselves on the

Sabbath; having found it, we immediately want to share it with others.

Human history, however, is replete with examples of the opposite of shalom. We have had world wars, wars between states, and wars on terror, hunger, and poverty. We have had threats of nuclear war, a Cold War, and a Hundred Years' War. Domestic wars now claim half of all marriages. On Sabbath, Nancy chooses to end, mitigate, and prevent the longest-running conflict in history. She takes on the war between the sexes.

Many men cheat on their spouses, but Nancy believes that more women cheat on their marriages. They withhold love from the person God has joined them to; they say no to their husbands. A wife is the only legitimate source of physical connecting a man should have in his life. "Sex delayed is sex denied," she says in a parody of the saying about justice. Her views on what to do on Sabbath are common among everyone from Pilgrims to Calvinists to Jewish teachers of old. Blessed be the peacemakers!

Finding God on the Other Side of Boredom

Charles Dickens did much to bring social ills to light. He also coined the term *boredom* and brought it into the world in his novel *Bleak House*. On several occasions when discussing the Sabbath, I've been confronted with negative, visceral reactions. "I grew up in Texas, and we couldn't even play ball on Sundays. Sundays were boring," one man complained.

Many people describe a feeling of dread and anxiety when they think about spending time in quiet or alone. They can't imagine going twenty-four hours without a connection to electronic media. If they disconnect for even an hour, they experience boredom.

I believe there are several reasons to deal with boredom and not simply mask it with entertainment. First, simply covering boredom and anxiety with distraction and entertainment is a losing battle. What passes for distraction today will need to be escalated tomorrow. More and more time will be spent distracting oneself with social media, playing computer games, and so on. Second, I believe the negative emotions and feelings we experience when we come to a stop are a barometer of our comfort with God. Are we truly bored by being alone with God in the midst of his glorious creation? Perhaps it is not God, the times, or the world that are boring. Maybe it is us. My advice is to wait in the stillness and boredom for the first sounds of the Lord's voice.

I am not saying that playing games of solitaire, watching golf on TV, or using an Xbox is evil or even wrong. But those types of activities need to be balanced by listening to the Lord. If you don't take the time to listen, how will you discern what the Lord is saying? Is the Lord really telling you that you were made to spend thousands of hours watching mindless entertainment? Deal with boredom: God is on the other side. Maybe a little boredom on Sabbaths is one of the points of the day.

Sabbaticals and Retreats

When I talked at the Chicago Opera House on the topic of 24/6, two interesting things happened. First, David, one of the attendees, got the word *REST* tattooed in three-inch block letters across his chest—in reverse. He is a Grammy-winning artist and a workaholic. He took the message to heart. He also started carrying a phone that only his wife and the sitter could call. His phone is the electronic version of the one that once inhabited your great-grandparents' kitchen. It places phone calls and does nothing else—no text messages, no videos, no Internet access.

When Nancy and I last spent time with David, his wife, Kate, said that the phone and the attempts at 24/6 were making a difference in their lives. I didn't ask about the effectiveness of David's seeing "REST" in the mirror each morning as he shaved, nor did I ask Kate what effect seeing "TƧƎЯ" was having on her.

Which brings me to the second thing that happened after the 24/6 talk. I got to know Jeremy Blume and learned about his firm's sabbatical philosophy. Jeremy is part of the DeMoss Group, a public relations firm that works for Christians and nonprofits. They represent folks like Billy Graham and the American Bible Society. Jeremy grew up as a preacher's kid and inherited a strong work ethic from his father. After he graduated from the University of North Carolina, he started working and has never stopped—except when he goes on sabbatical. His firm gives employees one month off every five years. This comes in addition to vacations. On Jeremy's two sabbaticals, he has traveled and thought about the meaning of God in his life.

He says that some of the DeMoss Group's clients can't understand this commitment to rest. Why doesn't the company just figure out what the sabbatical time is worth and write out a check? Why let employees take so much time off? Jeremy says that the company's leaders strongly discourage employees on sabbatical from checking in with clients or having any work-related contact. "They just mail us checks during sabbaticals," he says.

Many employees on sabbatical choose to travel to places that take them outside their normal sphere of activities. Jeremy said that on his first day away, his hand automatically reached to find a cell phone in the morning. The next morning he also reached instinctively, but caught himself. By the third morning, he thought about connecting but didn't reach. Instead, he reflected on building a margin in his life for God. He realized that much of his identity was based on what he did and not who he was.

The DeMoss Group has had one person on sabbatical decide that he was in the wrong line of work. When he came back, he got another job with the blessing of the firm. But almost without exception, the sabbatical system has led to a more stabilized and contented workforce.

"The worst thing about going on sabbatical is the first day back," Jeremy relates. "So many things we worry about are made trivial by the perspective of being away." We can describe this priority setting with biblical phrases such as "separating the wheat from the chaff" and "straining out a gnat and swallowing a camel." The tyranny of the urgent, business deals, and social distractions (like Facebook?) were all cited by those who walked away from Jesus.

The tyranny of the urgent, business deals, and social distractions were all cited by those who walked away from Jesus.

Sabbaticals, retreats, and pilgrimages are not compatible with a 24/7 world. Yet those who do make time for these pursuits find them to be among life's most meaningful moments. There is much wisdom in the saying, "No one reaches the end of life and regrets not having spent more time at the office."

"Behold, I Am Making All Things New"

One beautiful fall morning, I finished a twenty-four-hour shift in the emergency department and drove home. At the time, we still lived in an idyllic seaside village on the Maine coast. It was a Tuesday, and the kids were at school. The air was clear, and I lay on the couch in our family room, thinking, *Should I try to take a nap now or go to bed early tonight?*

After catching me up on home life and listening to me share stories from work, Nancy had walked over to our little post office to get the mail. I drifted off but woke up when she came back in. "Vince at the post office told me that a plane crashed into a building in New York." She turned on the news, and we watched with the rest of the country as the tragedy of 9/11 unfolded.

Our phone rang; Nancy answered it and handed it to me, saying, "Matthew, it's Liza. She needs to talk to you." Liza was Jamie's mother, and Jamie was our son Clark's friend from three houses away. Liza knew that, unfortunately, I had experience sharing bad news, and this morning she had horrific news: Jamie's dad had been in the first plane to hit the World Trade Center. Could I come over and help her tell Jamie that his dad was dead?

Later we got another call. Nancy's friend in DC had a brother and a husband at the Pentagon. Her brother had been killed. Her husband was safe, but he was being taken to Connecticut and would immediately be put to sea commanding a submarine. She would be alone at home to deal with her brother's death, grieving parents, and a new baby. In a few days, I left to go and visit. But for the rest of that Tuesday we were stunned and stayed put.

Many thousands of people have similar stories and recollections about that day. Americans responded generously. We gave blood, donated money, and prayed.

And a less obvious thing happened: the world, strangely, grew more peaceful. The sky became devoid of planes. People stayed home more. They let each other cut in line. The hospital system I was attached to suffered dramatic economic losses—not because people had lost their jobs or their insurance; that hadn't occurred yet. The hospital's bottom line suffered because people weren't coming to the hospital as much. For a month or two, because our thoughts were on others and not ourselves, we were healthier.

In the years following that September morning, I found God, meaning, and purpose. Many of these discoveries took place through our honoring the Fourth Commandment. Some things still don't make sense to me. But I do not think the Bible tells us that we can figure out all of life. That is the false hope of those who go 24/7.

In adopting a 24/6 life, we put God back into the equation. We leave some of the figuring out to him. We recharge our batteries with the energy that comes only through stopping, and we become more generous with the gifts God has given to us.

Life is serious business. It is not a matter of *if* hard times will come but *when*. In my brief lifetime, many more around the globe will be hit by earthquakes, tidal waves, and war. And all of us will be hit with the personal tragedies of death, betrayal, and loss.

When such hard times come, I wish you the power, resilience, and purpose that come from Sabbath rest. I pray that you are blessed with the faith, hope, and love found in the 24/6 life.

May the Lord bless you and keep you all the days of your life, but most especially on your day of rest.

I wish you the peace that passes all understanding: Shabbat shalom.

24/6 Scripture

The creation of the heavens and the earth and everything in them was completed. On the seventh day God had finished his work of creation, so he rested from all his work. And God blessed the seventh day and declared it holy, because it was the day when he rested from all his work of creation.

GENESIS 2:1-3

The LORD appeared again to Abraham near the oak grove belonging to Mamre. One day Abraham was sitting at the entrance to his tent during the hottest part of the day. He looked up and noticed three men standing nearby. When he saw them, he ran to meet them and welcomed them, bowing low to the ground.

"My lord," he said, "if it pleases you, stop here for a while. Rest in the shade of this tree while water is brought to wash your feet. And since you've honored your servant with this visit, let me prepare some food to refresh you before you continue on your journey."

"All right," they said. "Do as you have said."

So Abraham ran back to the tent and said to Sarah, "Hurry! Get three large measures of your best flour, knead it into dough, and bake some bread." Then Abraham ran out to the herd and chose a tender calf and gave it to his servant, who quickly prepared it. When the food was ready, Abraham took some yogurt and milk and the roasted meat, and he served it to the men. As they ate, Abraham waited on them in the shade of the trees.

GENESIS 18:1-8

The LORD asked Moses, "How long will these people refuse to obey my commands and instructions? They must realize that the Sabbath is the LORD's gift to you. That is why he gives you a two-day supply [of manna] on the sixth day, so there will be enough for two days. On the Sabbath day you must each stay in your place. Do not go out to pick up food on the seventh day."

EXODUS 16:28-29

Remember to observe the Sabbath day by keeping it holy. You have six days each week for your ordinary work, but the seventh day is a Sabbath day of rest dedicated to the LORD your God. On that day no one in your household may do any work. This includes you, your sons and daughters, your male and female servants, your livestock, and any foreigners living among you. For in six days the LORD made the heavens, the earth, the sea, and everything in them; but on the seventh day he rested. That is why the LORD blessed the Sabbath day and set it apart as holy.

EXODUS 20:8-11

Tell the people of Israel: "Be careful to keep my Sabbath day, for the Sabbath is a sign of the covenant between me and you from generation to generation. It is given so you may know that I am the LORD, who makes you holy. You must keep the Sabbath day, for it is a holy day for you. . . . The people of Israel must keep the Sabbath day by observing it from generation to generation. This is a covenant obligation for all time."

EXODUS 31:13-14, 16

You have six days each week for your ordinary work, but the seventh day is a Sabbath day of complete rest, an official day for holy assembly. It is the LORD's Sabbath day, and it must be observed wherever you live.

LEVITICUS 23:3

While Moses was on Mount Sinai, the LORD said to him, "Give the following instructions to the people of Israel. When you have entered the land I am giving you, the land itself must observe a Sabbath rest before the LORD every seventh year. For six years you may plant your fields and prune your vineyards and harvest your crops, but during the seventh year the land must have a Sabbath year of complete rest. It is the LORD's Sabbath. Do not plant your fields or prune your vineyards during that year. And don't store away the crops that grow on their own or gather the grapes from your unpruned vines. The land must have a year of complete rest. But you may eat whatever the land produces on its own during its Sabbath. This applies to you, your male and female servants, your hired workers, and the temporary residents who live with you. Your livestock and the wild animals in your land will also be allowed to eat what the land produces.

"In addition, you must count off seven Sabbath years, seven sets of seven years, adding up to forty-nine years in all. Then on the Day of Atonement in the fiftieth year, blow the ram's horn loud and long throughout the land. Set this year apart as holy, a time to proclaim freedom throughout the land for all who live there. It will be a jubilee year for you, when each of you may return to the land that belonged to your ancestors and return to your own clan. This fiftieth year will be a jubilee for you. During that year you must not plant your fields or store away any of the crops that grow on their own, and don't gather the grapes from your unpruned vines. It will be a jubilee year for you, and you must keep it holy. But you may eat whatever the land produces on its own. In the Year of Jubilee each of you may return to the land that belonged to your ancestors.

"When you make an agreement with your neighbor to buy or sell property, you must not take advantage of each other. When you buy land from your neighbor, the price you pay must be based on the number of years since the last jubilee. The seller must set the price by taking into account the number of years remaining until the next Year of Jubilee. The more years until the next jubilee, the higher the price; the fewer years, the lower the price. After all, the person selling the land is actually selling you a certain number of harvests."

LEVITICUS 25:1-16

In the Year of Jubilee the field must be returned to the person from whom he purchased it, the one who inherited it as family property.

LEVITICUS 27:24

Remember that you were once slaves in Egypt, but the LORD your God brought you out with his strong hand and powerful arm. That is why the LORD your God has commanded you to rest on the Sabbath day.

DEUTERONOMY 5:15

The message of the LORD spoken through Jeremiah was fulfilled. The land finally enjoyed its Sabbath rest, lying desolate until the seventy years were fulfilled, just as the prophet had said.

2 CHRONICLES 36:21

The rest of the people . . . joined their leaders and bound themselves with an oath. They swore a curse on themselves if they failed to obey the Law of God as issued by his servant Moses. They solemnly promised to carefully follow all the commands, regulations, and decrees of the LORD our Lord: . . . "We also promise that if the people of the land should bring any merchandise or grain to be sold on the Sabbath or on any other holy day, we will refuse to buy it. Every seventh year we will let our land rest, and we will cancel all debts owed to us."

NEHEMIAH 10:28-29, 31

I [Nehemiah] confronted the nobles of Judah. "Why are you profaning the Sabbath in this evil way?" I asked. "Wasn't it just this sort of thing that your ancestors did that caused our God to bring all this trouble upon us and our city? Now you are bringing even more wrath upon Israel by permitting the Sabbath to be desecrated in this way!"

Then I commanded that the gates of Jerusalem should be shut as darkness fell every Friday evening, not to be opened until the Sabbath ended. I sent some of my own servants to guard the gates so that no merchandise could be brought in on the Sabbath day. The merchants and tradesmen with a variety of wares camped outside Jerusalem once or twice. But I spoke sharply to them and said, "What are you doing out here, camping around the wall? If you do this again, I will arrest you!" And that was the last time they came on the Sabbath. Then I commanded the Levites to purify themselves and to guard the gates in order to preserve the holiness of the Sabbath.

NEHEMIAH 13:17-22

The LORD is my shepherd;
    I have all that I need.
He lets me rest in green meadows;
    he leads me beside peaceful streams.
    He renews my strength.
He guides me along right paths,
    bringing honor to his name.
Even when I walk
    through the darkest valley,

I will not be afraid,
  for you are close beside me.
Your rod and your staff
  protect and comfort me.
You prepare a feast for me
  in the presence of my enemies.
You honor me by anointing my head with oil.
  My cup overflows with blessings.
Surely your goodness and unfailing love will pursue me
  all the days of my life,
and I will live in the house of the LORD
  forever.

PSALM 23

Lord, through all the generations
  you have been our home!
Before the mountains were born,
  before you gave birth to the earth and the world,
  from beginning to end, you are God.

You turn people back to dust, saying,
  "Return to dust, you mortals!"
For you, a thousand years are as a passing day,
  as brief as a few night hours.
You sweep people away like dreams that disappear.
  They are like grass that springs up in the morning.

In the morning it blooms and flourishes,
>   but by evening it is dry and withered.
We wither beneath your anger;
>   we are overwhelmed by your fury.
You spread out our sins before you—
>   our secret sins—and you see them all.
We live our lives beneath your wrath,
>   ending our years with a groan.

Seventy years are given to us!
>   Some even live to eighty.
But even the best years are filled with pain and trouble;
>   soon they disappear, and we fly away.
Who can comprehend the power of your anger?
>   Your wrath is as awesome as the fear you deserve.
Teach us to realize the brevity of life,
>   so that we may grow in wisdom.

O LORD, come back to us!
>   How long will you delay?
>   Take pity on your servants!
Satisfy us each morning with your unfailing love,
>   so we may sing for joy to the end of our lives.
Give us gladness in proportion to our former misery!
>   Replace the evil years with good.
Let us, your servants, see you work again;
>   let our children see your glory.

And may the Lord our God show us his approval
and make our efforts successful.
Yes, make our efforts successful!

PSALM 90

This is what the LORD says:

"Be just and fair to all.
Do what is right and good,
for I am coming soon to rescue you
and to display my righteousness among you.
Blessed are all those
who are careful to do this.
Blessed are those who honor my Sabbath days of rest
and keep themselves from doing wrong.

"Don't let foreigners who commit themselves to the LORD say,
'The LORD will never let me be part of his people.'
And don't let the eunuchs say,
'I'm a dried-up tree with no children and no future.'
For this is what the LORD says:
I will bless those eunuchs
who keep my Sabbath days holy
and who choose to do what pleases me
and commit their lives to me.
I will give them—within the walls of my house—
a memorial and a name
far greater than sons and daughters could give.

For the name I give them is an everlasting one.
  It will never disappear!

"I will also bless the foreigners who commit themselves to the
    LORD,
  who serve him and love his name,
who worship him and do not desecrate the Sabbath day of rest,
  and who hold fast to my covenant.
I will bring them to my holy mountain of Jerusalem
  and will fill them with joy in my house of prayer.
I will accept their burnt offerings and sacrifices,
  because my Temple will be called a house of prayer for all
    nations.
For the Sovereign LORD,
  who brings back the outcasts of Israel, says:
I will bring others, too,
  besides my people Israel."

ISAIAH 56:1-8

Keep the Sabbath day holy.
  Don't pursue your own interests on that day,
but enjoy the Sabbath
  and speak of it with delight as the LORD's holy day.
Honor the Sabbath in everything you do on that day,
  and don't follow your own desires or talk idly.

ISAIAH 58:13

Say to all the people, "Listen to this message from the LORD, you
kings of Judah and all you people of Judah and everyone living

in Jerusalem. This is what the LORD says: Listen to my warning! Stop carrying on your trade at Jerusalem's gates on the Sabbath day. Do not do your work on the Sabbath, but make it a holy day. I gave this command to your ancestors, but they did not listen or obey. They stubbornly refused to pay attention or accept my discipline.

"But if you obey me, says the LORD, and do not carry on your trade at the gates or work on the Sabbath day, and if you keep it holy, then kings and their officials will go in and out of these gates forever. There will always be a descendant of David sitting on the throne here in Jerusalem. Kings and their officials will always ride in and out among the people of Judah in chariots and on horses, and this city will remain forever. And from all around Jerusalem, from the towns of Judah and Benjamin, from the western foothills and the hill country and the Negev, the people will come with their burnt offerings and sacrifices. They will bring their grain offerings, frankincense, and thanksgiving offerings to the LORD's Temple.

"But if you do not listen to me and refuse to keep the Sabbath holy, and if on the Sabbath day you bring loads of merchandise through the gates of Jerusalem just as on other days, then I will set fire to these gates. The fire will spread to the palaces, and no one will be able to put out the roaring flames."

JEREMIAH 17:20-27

I gave them my Sabbath days of rest as a sign between them and me. It was to remind them that I am the LORD, who had set them apart to be holy.

But the people of Israel rebelled against me, and they refused to obey my decrees there in the wilderness. They wouldn't obey my regulations even though obedience would have given them life. They also violated my Sabbath days. So I threatened to pour out my fury on them, and I made plans to utterly consume them in the wilderness.

EZEKIEL 20:12-13

Keep my Sabbath days holy, for they are a sign to remind you that I am the LORD your God.

EZEKIEL 20:20

Jesus said, "Come to me, all of you who are weary and carry heavy burdens, and I will give you rest. Take my yoke upon you. Let me teach you, because I am humble and gentle at heart, and you will find rest for your souls. For my yoke is easy to bear, and the burden I give you is light."

MATTHEW 11:28-30

Jesus was walking through some grainfields on the Sabbath. His disciples were hungry, so they began breaking off some heads of grain and eating them. But some Pharisees saw them do it and protested, "Look, your disciples are breaking the law by harvesting grain on the Sabbath."

Jesus said to them, "Haven't you read in the Scriptures what David did when he and his companions were hungry? He went into the house of God, and he and his companions broke the law by eating the sacred loaves of bread that only the priests are allowed to eat. And haven't you read in the law of Moses that the priests on duty in the Temple may work on the Sabbath? I tell you, there is one here who is even greater than the Temple! But you would not have condemned my innocent disciples if you knew the meaning of this Scripture: 'I want you to show mercy, not offer sacrifices.' For the Son of Man is Lord, even over the Sabbath!"

MATTHEW 12:1-8

Jesus went into the synagogue again and noticed a man with a deformed hand. Since it was the Sabbath, Jesus' enemies watched him closely. If he healed the man's hand, they planned to accuse him of working on the Sabbath.

Jesus said to the man with the deformed hand, "Come and stand in front of everyone." Then he turned to his critics and asked, "Does the law permit good deeds on the Sabbath, or is it a day for doing evil? Is this a day to save life or to destroy it?" But they wouldn't answer him.

He looked around at them angrily and was deeply saddened by their hard hearts. Then he said to the man, "Hold out your hand." So the man held out his hand, and it was restored! At once the Pharisees went away and met with the supporters of Herod to plot how to kill Jesus.

MARK 3:1-6

Jesus returned to Galilee, filled with the Holy Spirit's power. Reports about him spread quickly through the whole region. He taught regularly in their synagogues and was praised by everyone.

When he came to the village of Nazareth, his boyhood home, he went as usual to the synagogue on the Sabbath and stood up to read the Scriptures. The scroll of Isaiah the prophet was handed to him. He unrolled the scroll and found the place where this was written:

> "The Spirit of the LORD is upon me,
>> for he has anointed me to bring Good News to the poor.
> He has sent me to proclaim that captives will be released,
>> that the blind will see,
> that the oppressed will be set free,
>> and that the time of the LORD's favor has come."

He rolled up the scroll, handed it back to the attendant, and sat down. All eyes in the synagogue looked at him intently. Then he began to speak to them. "The Scripture you've just heard has been fulfilled this very day!"

LUKE 4:14-21

One Sabbath day as Jesus was teaching in a synagogue, he saw a woman who had been crippled by an evil spirit. She had been bent double for eighteen years and was unable to stand up straight. When Jesus saw her, he called her over and said, "Dear woman, you are healed of your sickness!" Then he touched her, and instantly she could stand straight. How she praised God!

But the leader in charge of the synagogue was indignant that Jesus had healed her on the Sabbath day. "There are six days of the week for working," he said to the crowd. "Come on those days to be healed, not on the Sabbath."

But the Lord replied, "You hypocrites! Each of you works on the Sabbath day! Don't you untie your ox or your donkey from its stall on the Sabbath and lead it out for water? This dear woman, a daughter of Abraham, has been held in bondage by Satan for eighteen years. Isn't it right that she be released, even on the Sabbath?"

LUKE 13:10-16

Jesus replied, "I did one miracle on the Sabbath, and you were amazed. But you work on the Sabbath, too, when you obey Moses' law of circumcision. (Actually, this tradition of circumcision began with the patriarchs, long before the law of Moses.) For if the correct time for circumcising your son falls on the Sabbath, you go ahead and do it so as not to break the law of Moses. So why should you be angry with me for healing a man on the Sabbath? Look beneath the surface so you can judge correctly."

JOHN 7:21-24

Some think one day is more holy than another day, while others think every day is alike. You should each be fully convinced that whichever day you choose is acceptable. Those who worship the Lord on a special day do it to honor him. Those who eat any kind of food do so to honor the Lord, since they give thanks to God before eating. And those who refuse to eat certain foods also want to please the Lord and give thanks to God. For we don't live for ourselves or die for ourselves. If we live, it's to honor the Lord. And if we die, it's to honor the Lord. So whether we live or die, we belong to the Lord. Christ died and rose again for this very purpose—to be Lord both of the living and of the dead.

So why do you condemn another believer? Why do you look down on another believer? Remember, we will all stand before the judgment seat of God. For the Scriptures say,

"As surely as I live,' says the LORD,
'every knee will bend to me,
    and every tongue will confess and give praise to God.'"

Yes, each of us will give a personal account to God. So let's stop condemning each other. Decide instead to live in such a way that you will not cause another believer to stumble and fall.

ROMANS 14:5-13

Regarding your question about the money being collected for God's people in Jerusalem. You should follow the same procedure I gave to the churches in Galatia. On the first day of each week, you should each put aside a portion of the money you have earned. Don't wait until I get there and then try to collect it all at once.

1 CORINTHIANS 16:1-2

God is the one who provides seed for the farmer and then bread to eat. In the same way, he will provide and increase your resources and then produce a great harvest of generosity in you.

Yes, you will be enriched in every way so that you can always be generous. And when we take your gifts to those who need them, they will thank God.

2 CORINTHIANS 9:10-11

God's promise of entering his rest still stands, so we ought to tremble with fear that some of you might fail to experience it. For this good news—that God has prepared this rest—has been announced to us just as it was to them. But it did them no good because they didn't share the faith of those who listened to God.

For only we who believe can enter his rest. As for the others, God said,

> *"In my anger I took an oath:*
>   *'They will never enter my place of rest,'"*

even though this rest has been ready since he made the world. We know it is ready because of the place in the Scriptures where it mentions the seventh day: "On the seventh day God rested from all his work." But in the other passage God said, "They will never enter my place of rest."

So God's rest is there for people to enter, but those who first heard this good news failed to enter because they disobeyed God. So God set another time for entering his rest, and that time is today. God announced this through David much later in the words already quoted:

> *"Today when you hear his voice,*
>   *don't harden your hearts."*

Now if Joshua had succeeded in giving them this rest, God would not have spoken about another day of rest still to come. So there is a special rest still waiting for the people of God. For all who have entered into God's rest have rested from their labors, just as God did after creating the world. So let us do our best to enter that rest. But if we disobey God, as the people of Israel did, we will fall.

For the word of God is alive and powerful. It is sharper than the sharpest two-edged sword, cutting between soul and spirit, between joint and marrow. It exposes our innermost thoughts and desires. Nothing in all creation is hidden from God.

Everything is naked and exposed before his eyes, and he is the one to whom we are accountable.

HEBREWS 4:1-13

Don't forget to show hospitality to strangers, for some who have done this have entertained angels without realizing it!

HEBREWS 13:2

Then the angel showed me a river with the water of life, clear as crystal, flowing from the throne of God and of the Lamb. It flowed down the center of the main street. On each side of the river grew a tree of life, bearing twelve crops of fruit, with a fresh crop each month. The leaves were used for medicine to heal the nations.

No longer will there be a curse upon anything. For the throne of God and of the Lamb will be there, and his servants will worship him. And they will see his face, and his name will be written on their foreheads. And there will be no night there—no need for lamps or sun—for the Lord God will shine on them. And they will reign forever and ever.

Then the angel said to me, "Everything you have heard and seen is trustworthy and true. The Lord God, who inspires his prophets, has sent his angel to tell his servants what will happen soon."

REVELATION 22:1-6

24/6 Quotes

To live well is to work well, to show a good activity.
Thomas Aquinas

Thou madest us for Thyself, and our heart is restless, until it rests in Thee.
Augustine of Hippo

Has it ever struck you that the trouts bite best on the Sabbath? God's critturs tempting decent men.
James Matthew Barrie

A being is free only when it can determine and limit its activity.
Karl Barth

A world without a Sabbath would be like a man without a smile, like a summer without flowers, and like a homestead without a garden. It is the joyous day of the whole week.
Henry Ward Beecher

The savings bank of human existence is the weekly Sabbath.
   William Garden Blaikie

I feel as if God had, by giving the Sabbath, given fifty-two springs in each year.
   Samuel Taylor Coleridge

Sabbath ceasing [means] to cease not only from work itself, but also from the need to accomplish and be productive, from the worry and tension that accompany our modern criterion of efficiency, from our efforts to be in control of our lives as if we were God, from our possessiveness and our enculturation, and, finally, from the humdrum and meaninglessness that result when life is pursued without the Lord at the center of it all.
   Marva J. Dawn

The Sunday is the core of our civilization, dedicated to thought and reverence. It invites to the noblest solitude and to the noblest society.
   Ralph Waldo Emerson

He who cannot rest, cannot work; he who cannot let go, cannot hold on; he who cannot find footing, cannot go forward.
   Harry Emerson Fosdick

It would be as difficult to take an inventory of the benefits the world receives from the sunshine as to enumerate the blessings we derive from the Christian Sabbath.
   Hervey Doddridge Ganse

The streams of religion run deep or shallow, according as the banks of the Sabbath are kept up or neglected.

Matthew Henry

I think the world of today would go mad, just frenzied with strain and pressure, but for the blessed institution of Sunday.

Brooke Herford

He who ordained the Sabbath loves the poor.

Oliver Wendell Holmes

It comes the very moment you wake up each morning. All your wishes and hopes for the day rush at you like wild animals. And the first job each morning consists simply in shoving them all back; in listening to that other voice, taking that other point of view, letting that other larger, stronger, quieter life come flowing in. And so on, all day. Standing back from all your natural fussings and frettings; coming in out of the wind.

C. S. Lewis

As we keep or break the Sabbath day, we nobly save or meanly lose the last best hope by which man rises.

Abraham Lincoln

Sunday is the golden clasp that binds together the volume of the week.

Henry Wadsworth Longfellow

The spiritual rest, which God particularly intends in this Commandment, is this: that we not only cease from our labor and trade, but much more, that we let God alone work in us and that we do nothing of our own with all our powers.

Martin Luther

I have not the smallest doubt that, if we and our ancestors had, during the last three centuries, worked just as hard on the Sunday as on the week days, we should have been at this moment a poorer people and a less civilised people than we are.

Thomas Babington Macaulay

A believer longs after God—to come into his presence—to feel his love—to feel near to him in secret—to feel in the crowd that he is nearer than all the creatures. Ah! dear brethren, have you ever tasted this blessedness? There is greater rest and solace to be found in the presence of God for one hour than in an eternity of the presence of man.

Robert Murray McCheyne

Where there is no Christian Sabbath, there is no Christian morality; and without this, free institutions cannot long be sustained.

John McLean

When your tongue is silent, you can rest in the silence of the forest. When your imagination is silent, the forest speaks to you. It tells you of its unreality and of the Reality of God. But when your mind is silent, then the forest suddenly becomes magnificently real and blazes transparently with the Reality of God.

Thomas Merton

Without a Sabbath, no worship; without worship, no religion; and without religion, no permanent freedom.

Charles Forbes Montalembert

Like a path through the forest, Sabbath creates a marker for ourselves so, if we are lost, we can find our way back to our center.

Wayne Muller

I never knew a man to escape failure, in either body or mind, who worked seven days in the week.

Sir Robert Peel

Sabbath is that uncluttered time and space in which we can distance ourselves from our own activities enough to see what God is doing.

Eugene Peterson

If once a man indulges himself in murder, very soon he comes to think little of robbing, and from robbing he next comes to drinking and Sabbath-breaking, and from that to incivility and procrastination.

Thomas De Quincey

The green oasis, the little grassy meadow in the wilderness, where, after the week-day's journey, the pilgrim halts for refreshment and repose.

Charles Reade

Do not let Sunday be taken from you. If your soul has no Sunday, it becomes an orphan.

Albert Schweitzer

The bow cannot be always bent without fear of breaking. Repose is as needful to the mind as sleep to the body. . . . Rest time is not waste time. It is economy to gather fresh strength. . . . It is wisdom to take occasional furlough. In the long run, we shall do more by sometimes doing less.

Charles Spurgeon

Money gained on Sabbath-day is a loss, I dare to say. No blessing can come with that which comes to us, on the devil's back, by our willful disobedience of God's law. The loss of health by neglect of rest, and the loss of soul by neglect of hearing the gospel, soon turn all seeming profit into real loss.

Charles Spurgeon

In place of our exhaustion and spiritual fatigue, He will give us rest. All He asks is that we come to Him . . . that we spend a while thinking about Him, meditating on him, talking to Him, listening in silence, occupying ourselves with Him—totally and thoroughly lost in the hiding place of His presence.

Chuck Swindoll

He that remembers not to keep the Christian Sabbath at the beginning of the week, will be in danger of forgetting, before the end of the week, that he is a Christian.

Sir Edward Turner

Break down Sunday, close the churches, open the bars and the theatres on that day, and where would values be?—What was real estate worth in Sodom?

Heman Lincoln Wayland

The longer I live, the more highly do I estimate the importance of a proper observance of the Christian Sabbath, and the more grateful do I feel towards those who take pains to impress a sense of this importance on the community.

Daniel Webster

O what a blessing is Sunday, interposed between the waves of worldly business like the divine path of the Israelites through the sea! There is nothing in which I would advise you to be more strictly conscientious than in keeping the Sabbath day holy. I can truly declare that to me the Sabbath has been invaluable.

William Wilberforce

He that would prepare for heaven, must honour the Sabbath upon earth.

David Wilson

The Sabbath is the link between the paradise which has passed away and the paradise which is yet to come.

Andrew Wylie

24/6 Blessings

I HEAR so many curses in this world. We all hear them, everywhere. But God gave us an antidote: "blessings."

Thousands of years ago, the Hebrew people developed a vocabulary of blessings. They created blessings for when it rains, when lightning strikes, and when a rainbow fills the sky. They penned blessings for smelling the fragrant woods and watching the first blossom unfold. And they created special blessings for the Sabbath day.

Following are a few blessings you may wish to incorporate into your Sabbath practices. Blessing a child, loved one, or enemy changes the calculus of the world. Start with blessings on your Sabbath, and then let them flow into the other days and nights of your week.

May the Lord bless you and keep you. May you see falling stars and hear children sing. May you find rest for your soul and touch the robe of God.

BLESSING OVER THE CANDLES

To welcome the Sabbath, observant Jews light two candles representing the two primary commands about Shabbat: "Remember the Sabbath" (Exodus 20:8, ESV) and "Observe the Sabbath" (Deuteronomy 5:12).

English: Blessed are you, Lord our God, King of the universe, who has made us holy through his commandments and commanded us to kindle the Sabbath light.

Transliteration from Hebrew: *Barukh atah Adonai Eloheinu, melekh ha'olam, asher kid'shanu b'mitzvotav v'tzivanu l'hadlik ner shel Shabbat.*

BLESSING OVER RITUAL WASHING OF THE HANDS

Pouring water over the hands is a symbolic way of washing away the worldly cares of the week and entering into the holiness of Sabbath rest.

English: Blessed are you, Lord our God, King of the universe, who has sanctified us with his commandments and commanded us concerning washing of hands.

Transliteration: *Barukh atah Adonai Eloheinu, melekh ha'olam, asher qiddeshanu b'mitzvotav v'tzivanu al netilath yadayim.*

BLESSING OVER THE BREAD

Traditionally, two loaves of challah (braided Jewish egg bread) are served, representing the two portions of manna the Jews were instructed to collect in the desert before the Sabbath.

English: Blessed are you, Lord our God, King of the universe, who brings forth bread from the earth.

Transliteration: *Barukh atah Adonai Eloheinu, melekh ha'olam, ha'motzi lehem min ha-aretz.*

BLESSING OVER THE WINE (OR GRAPE JUICE)

This blessing is traditionally said at both the beginning and the close of the Sabbath (the Havdalah service). In the Havdalah service, the cup is filled until it overflows onto a plate set below, representing our desire for Sabbath blessings to overflow into the coming week.

English: Blessed are you, Lord our God, King of the universe, Creator of the fruit of the vine.

Transliteration: *Barukh atah Adonai Eloheinu, melekh ha'olam, boray pri hagafen.*

BLESSING FOR A SON

The traditional blessing said over a son asks God to make him like Jacob's grandsons (Joseph's sons), Ephraim and Manasseh. Known for their good deeds, these brothers were true friends—not rivals like the biblical brothers who came before them.

English: May God make you like Ephraim and Manasseh.

Transliteration: *Ye'simcha Elohim ke-Ephraim ve hee-Menashe.*

BLESSING FOR A DAUGHTER
The blessing for daughters asks God to make them like Sarah, Rebekah, Rachel, and Leah. Despite many hardships, these four women put God and family first and became the matriarchs of the Jewish faith.

English: May God make you like Sarah, Rebekah, Rachel, and Leah.

Transliteration: *Ye'simech Elohim ke-Sarah, Rivka, Rachel ve-Leah.*

BLESSING FOR CHILDREN
Sometimes called the "priestly blessing," many families recite this additional blessing over both boys and girls.

English: May God bless you and protect you. May God's face shine toward you and show you favor. May God look favorably upon you and grant you peace.

Transliteration: *Ye'varech'echa Adonoy ve'yish'merecha. Ya'ir Adonoy panav eilecha viy-chuneka. Yisa Adonoy panav eilecha, ve'yasim lecha shalom.*

About the Author

DR. MATTHEW SLEETH serves as executive director of
a Christian educational nonprofit, Blessed Earth. He is
the author of *Serve God, Save the Planet: A Christian Call
to Action*, the introduction to *The Green Bible*, and the
Serving God, Saving the Planet film series. A former emergency room physician and hospital chief of staff, Dr. Sleeth
graduated from George Washington University School of
Medicine and has two postdoctoral fellowships.

Dr. Sleeth resides in Lexington, Kentucky, with Nancy,
his wife of more than thirty years. The Sleeths live near
their adult children, Clark (a physician married to Valerie,
both preparing for full-time medical missions) and Emma
(an Asbury University graduate and author).

ABOUT BLESSED EARTH

Blessed Earth is an educational nonprofit that inspires
and equips people of faith to become better stewards of
the earth. Through church, campus, and media outreach,

Blessed Earth builds bridges that promote measurable environmental change and meaningful spiritual growth. For additional Sabbath and creation care resources, please visit www.blessedearth.org.

READY TO TAKE THE NEXT STEP?

{ *Almost Amish* and *Go Green, Save Green* will help you simplify your life, strengthen your family, and grow in your faith! }

The perfect book for any woman looking to slow down, simplify, and get back to the things that matter most

A highly practical how-to guide to going green

Now available in stores and online